SO, YOU ARE GOING TO COLLEGE?!

THINGS YOU WISH YOU KNEW BEFORE HEADING TO CLASS

SECOND EDITION

by San Bolkan, PhD

California State University
Long Beach

San Diego, CA

First published in the United States of America in 2011 by Cognella, a division of University Readers, Inc.

15 14 13 12 11   1 2 3 4 5

Printed in the United States of America

ISBN: 978-1-60927-928-8

www.cognella.com 800.200.3908

Acknowledgments

T hanks to all my friends and family who have helped me get to where I am today. Writing this book was not an individual achievement. Only through community has this work been made possible. Thanks especially to Darrin Griffin who believed in this book and helped it become what it is. Also, Darrin drew the stick figures in the book.

Dedication

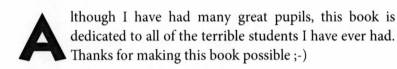

lthough I have had many great pupils, this book is dedicated to all of the terrible students I have ever had. Thanks for making this book possible ;-)

CONTENTS

CHAPTER TWO

BEFORE WE BEGIN

I bet you want to know why you should read this book.
Good, read on and let me tell you.

I am sure you are aware that college offers you terrific opportunities for personal growth. These occur both inside and outside the classroom. For instance, college offers opportunities to socialize with your peers, opportunities to travel and study abroad, and opportunities to join extracurricular groups. College is a great place to learn about the world and it is important that you use the experience to develop your potential and meet your goals.

Although there are a variety of things that are important to consider when it comes to college, this book focuses on one in particular: doing well in the classroom. I wrote this book to help explain what it takes to meet the expectations of your professors and succeed in your academic endeavors. Of course, because the book is designed to teach you what it takes to excel in your classes, there will be topics that I don't focus on. That's OK, I can't cover everything. Just know that this book was written for a specific purpose and when you read it think about how the information provided applies to the way you approach your studies.

You should also know that I designed this book to be concise. I bet you are excited about that. You should be. This book is brief and to the point for a few reasons. First, when I was a student I hated reading books that included fluff just to meet certain page requirements. I do not do that. When I am done saying something I may explain it in a different way to help illustrate an example, but I try to stay brief and to the point. Second, although I could talk about any one topic in this book forever, there is a point at which you would probably stop reading anyway. I cover a variety of topics in this book in an effort to get you thinking about school in a different light. If you want more in-depth information about a certain subject, consider reading a book dedicated to just that one. Third, this book was written to accompany a variety of courses. That is, what you have in front of you was not written to be a full-length textbook itself. If you are going to college you already have enough to read. To make you read another four hundred-page textbook about success in school in addition to the textbooks you already have—or will have—in your courses would be ridiculous.

Finally, because I know that students learn more when they like the material and when they like their teachers, I have tried to make this book a fun read. Part of my teaching philosophy is that learning should be enjoyable. In fact, some of my own research points to the notion that the more you like a class the more you learn, are motivated to learn, are satisfied with your communication with your teacher, and participate in class.[1] So, I hope you appreciate my efforts to make the book enjoyable and I hope that the tone of the book makes you want to read it—and, importantly, follow my advice. That is not to say there won't be important information in this book, there will be. It is just that instead of reading a book written by a stuffy professor, I want you to know that I made an effort to create a book that I would enjoy reading if I had to do it. I hope you like the book and I hope you learn a lot from it! Let the journey begin …

INTRODUCTION

INTRODUCTION

No book can start without a terrific introduction. So, let's begin with a preview of what's to come.

After graduating from college with a GPA of 3.83, then moving on to a master's program, a PhD program, and teaching at four-year universities for more than a decade, I can safely say that I know what it takes to succeed in the academic world. And it is my opinion that just about anybody can do well in school if he or she takes the right approach.

I say "just about anybody" because, in reality, some people do not have the ability to do well in a structured educational environment. That's fine, everyone is not created equal; some of us are better at some things and some of us are better at other things. Take me, for example. I am really good at a lot of things including being extremely strong and doing tons of pushups, being awesome and funny, Wii tennis, running long distances without stopping, and being a ridiculously good driver. Sure, those are a lot of great things that many people want to be good at, but there are other things that I am not so good at. These include swimming, diving off diving boards, running fast for short distances, getting good haircuts, and sleeping for an entire night without waking up at least once.

What is beautiful about not being great at everything is that this is normal. Some researchers suggest that to get good at something, and I mean genuinely good at something, you have to deliberately practice a skill for at least ten years.[2] That is a long time—and, really, that is what it takes to become proficient in a certain field. Considering that you have a finite time on Earth, you cannot hope to become an expert in everything you do. Instead, specializing in one thing and doing that well seems to make the most sense as far as your time management is concerned. Luckily, this setup works for us as humans because we can count on others to fill in where we need them (and vice versa). It is this exchange of services and resources that allows us to build communities and prosper. Think about it, if you had to build your house, stab a deer for food, cook the food, teach your kids, and put out fires you would be spread way too thin to do any one of these things well. Instead, we have construction engineers, food processors, grocers, teachers, and firefighters who do their respective jobs so that they can specialize and do well in that one thing. Then we barter, trade, share, and we all live happily ever after.

OK, all that was a long way of saying that we are not, in fact, equal in our abilities and we shouldn't want to be. We should celebrate our diversity and realize that it helps us to live happy lives. So, if you are a person who does not do well in school, don't force it. Figure out what you need to do to succeed in life and do that—some of the most successful people I know have never taken a single college course.

Although what I just wrote is true you should know that, statistically speaking, going to college is in your financial best interest. According to the U.S. Census Bureau,[3] over an average lifetime, people without high school diplomas will earn about $1 million, people with high school diplomas will earn about $1.2 million, and those with bachelor's degrees will earn about $2.1 million. And if you go on to get a master's degree you can expect to earn around $2.5 million in your lifetime. Moreover, if you look at average yearly salaries people with bachelor's degrees can expect to earn about $49,000 a year while those who settle for high school diplomas can expect to earn roughly $28,000 a year.

So remember, generally speaking, going to college will offer you a financial advantage over individuals who do not attend universities. And while some people won't do well in college, many will, and you can be one of these people. You simply need the skills to do well, the motivation to work hard, and the money to pay for the constantly rising tuition!

MY MOTIVATION

This book was created because, as a professor, I realized that while a lot of my students were smart and capable, they did not do well in school because they went about their educations in a fashion that did not lead to success. These students undermined their own achievement because they did not know what they needed to do to succeed in a college environment. However, I also realized that this was not my students' fault. My experience has shown me that knowing what it takes to do well in college is never learned in high school. And, really, it is never explicitly taught in college either. I wanted to change that. There are simple formulas for doing well in school and this book will give you some of them.

It is important that you learn these formulas because mastering them will help prepare you to face a multitude of situations in professional settings. Although this makes intuitive sense, a lot of my students fail to realize this in class. The rules you learn in school and the policies that professors have in their classrooms are meant to help train you for success in business environments. You need to understand and respect this. Professors do not have arbitrary rules to get you down. Instead, we are trying to help you learn the knowledge necessary to be successful once you leave college. For example, in my classes students sometimes get upset about my late assignments policy. They think it is unfair that they should lose points if an assignment is not completed on time or if they forgot it in their dorm rooms. The truth is I could accept late assignments for full credit. But if I did this my students would never learn from their mistakes. When you enter the business world people will not accept that you forgot your work at home or could not get it completed on time. It is better to learn this lesson in school where it will only cost you a few points than it is to learn it on the job where it may cost you a client or, even worse, your livelihood. The rules you learn and the skills you develop in college are not random; they are important for your survival outside of a university setting.

Because students need to know how to effectively navigate a university classroom, I set out to codify a few rules that will help you in your quest for a degree. If you follow the prescriptions I lay out in this book, I promise that you will be more successful in college (and in life) than if you do not. So read this book! Then, after you learn a ton of stuff and get a job you can thank me, give me a virtual high-five, and be proud of your accomplishment.

THE LAYOUT

I am a professor at California State University, Long Beach, and there is a saying printed on banners around campus that reads: "Graduation Begins Today." These banners are placed around school to help students understand that the things they are doing now and the decisions they are making today ultimately influence the futures they will have tomorrow. As you read the next one hundred something pages you will notice that the central message I am trying to communicate in this book is similar to one printed on the banners at my university. That is, instead of thinking of college as a four-year holding period between high school and your life as an adult, you need to see college as an important first step toward your success as a working professional. That said, you need to treat college as the first stage in your career and approach your studies in the same way you would approach any other job—in a mature, professional fashion.

Whether or not you have been exposed to information regarding what it takes to be a professional student, this book will help you learn what it takes to become one. The book will begin with a look at some of the myths students have about professors and about college in general. Yes, I said myths. I was a student once too and I know how you think. Now that I am a professor I know that a lot of the things students believe about their professors and about college are unwarranted. By reading this book you will learn some of the expectations professors have of their students and you will learn some of the behaviors you need to perform if you want to do well in college. This is important information because it is only after you know someone's expectations that you can hope to satisfy that person, which, generally speaking, can be done either by meeting or exceeding their expectations.[4]

Next, I will discuss the number 1 rule for success in life—being an adult. I will talk about how this idea applies in your life as a college student and how you can use your maturity and intelligence to have a successful academic career.

After I talk about how to be an adult, I will discuss some of the expectations professors have regarding their communication with students. Students often upset their professors without even knowing it because their communication with us is terrible. By simply changing the way you communicate with your professors you will change the way we think about you.

After the chapter on communication, I will focus on how to listen effectively in class. This information will do two things. First, it will help you learn more and daydream less. Second, it will help you understand the interactive nature of listening and the important role listeners play in healthy communication interactions.

Next, I will give you a formula for doing well on exams. Some of my students fail my tests and then wonder why. When I ask them how much they studied they reply, "Three hours." At that point I proceed to laugh and then wait to see if they are kidding. When they tell me they are not kidding I look at them disapprovingly and then close my eyes, hoping that they will disappear. I will teach you what it takes to do well on your exams, and believe me it takes more than simply looking at a book for three hours.

Finally, I will lay out a plan to help you become aware of your goals in college. You are here for a reason and you need to understand what that reason is. So, now that you know the layout of the book, you can choose what you want to do next. What will you do? Will you:

A) Get excited about learning what it takes to excel in college, read the book, and start becoming awesome?
B) Put the book down and challenge someone to a terrifying game of *World of Warcraft*?
C) Look me up on Facebook and *try* to befriend me?
D) Get going on your daily GTL (Gym, Tan, Laundry)?
E) Join an all men's yoga class?

CHAPTER ONE
MYTHS

MYTHS

1

Like urban legends, myths about college permeate university campuses. And, just like urban legends, they are usually not true, at all.

Many students come to college with unrealistic expectations about the way things work at universities. Often, these inaccurate beliefs are exacerbated by communication with other unenlightened individuals. Sometimes students' ideas about college are so far off the mark that it seems as if they and their professors are living in different realities. This is not a good thing. To do well in college it is important that you foster the ability to see your education from the same standpoint as your professors.

What you will find on the next few pages are a series of myths that I have put together in an attempt to align our worlds of experience. Of course, simply knowing the myths is not enough. Therefore, after each myth I tell you how to look at things from the perspective of your professors. Understanding this alternative point of view will help you do better when it comes to meeting our expectations and it will help you to have the right mind-set when it comes to succeeding in school. This is my gift to you—cherish it.

PROFESSORS ARE ULTIMATELY THE ONES WHO GIVE YOU YOUR GRADES

Wrong, professors are simply mirrors. Really, really, really smart mirrors that reflect your work back to you in the form of a letter grade. If you have ever had a job I want you to think about that experience and ask yourself if your boss ever *gave* you a paycheck. I bet the answer to that question is no, you have always had to earn your money. Well, the same is true in class. As professors, we do not *give* away anything. Instead, you *earn* your grades.

IN THE CLASSROOM, HARD WORK IS REWARDED

Nuh-uh. Let me explain why not with an example. If a water pipe burst in your house and water started leaking through your walls, one thing you could do is try to fix the issue yourself. You could work as hard as you wanted and you could even spend hours trying to correct the problem. But do you think that your sweat and tears are going to fix the leak by themselves? Of course not. The only things that will make a difference regarding whether your house gets flooded or not is your expertise in plumbing and your ability to do what it takes to stop the water. In this situation, your mastery of plumbing will be rewarded, not your effort in trying to resolve the dilemma. Your pipes don't care how hard you worked to fix the problem and your carpets aren't worried about how much effort you put into resolving the issue. All that matters in this case is whether you did the job right or not. The same is true in school. Even though you may have worked hard to do your best in a class or on an assignment, all that matters in the end is your mastery of the material presented in your courses.

People commonly mistake hard work for quality work, and this is especially true in ambiguous situations.[5] And because the quality of schoolwork can often be ambiguous (e.g., speeches, papers, etc.), you are particularly likely to mistake your hard work for a job well done. But remember this: just because you spent a lot of time—or put forth a lot of effort—on something does not necessarily mean that you did a good job with it. Although hard work is often associated with doing well in class, *this is not always the case*. In college, professors reward excellence, not effort.

PROFESSORS WANT TO KEEP GRADES LOW

This is not true. Your professors are dedicated to giving you an honest assessment of your performance based on your mastery of the material presented throughout their courses, we do not get rewarded for keeping grades low. There is no incentive for us to do this. In fact, students' evaluations of professors at the end of the semester may be more positive if grades are high![6]

Please know that professors do not love handing out grades, especially low grades. It is just that the university mandates that we give scores based on classroom performance. We have to do this. It is the *only* way that anybody who was not in class with us (which is pretty much everybody in the world) can examine how well you did in a certain area of study. We know you would all like to get A's but that is simply not going to happen very often.

If everybody got A's that would mean that everybody had mastered the material, and that rarely occurs. Besides, if everyone got A's then an A wouldn't be worth squat. Think of it this way, if you highlight an entire page in a book, nothing, in effect, is highlighted to stand out. Similarly, if everyone who walked into class got an A, your A would not be worth very much.

PROFESSORS CREATE THE CLASSROOM ATMOSPHERE

Wrong. Together with you, the students, we co-create the atmosphere in the classroom. Whenever I talk with my professor friends about this subject we all agree that classes are a lot like individuals: they all have their own unique personalities. While some classes are rambunctious, others are calm. Some classes are talkative and others are silent. Understand that the classroom atmosphere affects your professors' teaching styles as much as their teaching styles affect the classroom atmosphere.

That said, you possess the ability to have a major effect on the way your professors run their classes. If you want more discussion, start discussing things more. If you want more explanations, ask for them in class. Take an active role in creating a healthy classroom environment and be sure to seek the type of education you desire.

PROFESSORS ARE UNAPPROACHABLE

No way, Jose. Professors are just like you. In fact, people often consider us to be professional students. When you see your professors, realize that we have a lot of the same goals, pleasures, desires, and fears that you do … after all, we are human! Do not be afraid of professors and think that we are unapproachable. Instead, try to see us as people who are in a position to help educate you.

Moreover, do not be afraid to befriend your professors. Be sure to say hello if you happen to see us on the quad, in the gym, or at the supermarket. If you want to have a conversation with us, then ask us to lunch. You may be surprised to learn that professors are normal people and, just like you, we appreciate the extra effort you make to see us as such.

Two professors off to enjoy a day of skateboarding. See, we are just like you. Well, maybe we are a little bit tanner.

PROFESSORS LIKE TO CRITICIZE YOU

Nope. We do not like to do this. In fact, sometimes it is hard to do. However, our jobs require us to help you learn. And it takes making mistakes to figure out how to do something well. Let me give you an example. When I was a kid I used to love skiing. A few friends and I skied several times every winter. Looking back, I realize that my friends got much better at skiing than I did. Within a few years many of them could go down advanced runs while I was still rocking the bunny slopes. Interestingly, the difference between them and me did not necessarily lay in our true athletic abilities. Instead, the difference lay in our experiences. You see, because I was afraid to go down the advanced slopes I chose to avoid them. I was afraid of falling and hurting myself on the moguls and jumps that the harder trails required. But my friends did not share my fears. As a result, when they tried the harder trails they fell and got beat up. I remember making fun of them for whining about their bruises as we rode the chairlifts back up the mountains. However, it was by falling down and correcting their mistakes that my friends were able to learn and eventually improve. Years after we started at the same level, my friends were experts while I had not progressed in my skiing ability. In retrospect, I know that I never got better at skiing because I was unwilling to make mistakes.

The same principle is true in academics: you learn in school by making errors and then correcting them. And because it is your professors' job to let you know how to improve, we have to be honest with you and provide constructive criticism when it is warranted. That is, we have to point out when you fail. It may take thick skin to handle the criticism, but if professors never gave you feedback about how to improve, you would never know how to do it. Because you are in college to develop, you have to learn to welcome criticism instead of shielding yourself from it. And, in light of how learning from failure can lead to success, try not to take feedback personally. Instead, take the information and use it to do better in the classroom and also in life.

I can't wait to get home to grade students and make them feel bad about themselves!

← Sarcastic picture

AS LONG AS YOU TURN IN AN ASSIGNMENT, YOUR PROFESSOR SHOULD ACCEPT IT

No. For me to accept your assignment you need to turn it in to me in a professional manner. Instead of doing things the easy way, you need to do things the right way. For example, at the very least make sure that you type all of your assignments (unless specified otherwise) and be sure to staple your papers together. For whatever reason, this last part tends to be a problem for students. Last time I checked, staples were not made out of gold and I know for a fact that they are relatively easy to come by. So, do not simply print your papers and then turn them in. Staple them together. Do not bend a flap of paper over another flap of paper and think that your makeshift origami skills will work in place of a staple. Staple them. And do not show up to class and look at me as if it is my job to provide you with a stapler. Before class begins, get a stapler, and staple your assignment. Seriously. When I drive home from class and have your assignments in the back of my car I don't want a mess. And since I drive really fast with the windows rolled down (blasting '90s rap music), there is a good chance that your papers will fly everywhere when the wind catches them. If your papers are not stapled together I have to spend a lot of time in my garage figuring out whose paper belongs where. Then I get frustrated with you and your assignment. By the time I head to Costco in traffic to buy groceries for dinner and return to grade your paper I am in a doubly bad mood. Consequently, I link you to a negative emotional state for the rest of our time together. This is a bad thing.

Submitting papers that are handwritten, not stapled, or otherwise turned in inappropriately makes you seem rushed and unprofessional. Whether true or not, this makes it seem to your professors that you took very little time to complete your assignments. In the business world you would never dream of turning in a ten-page report to a client that was handwritten, not stapled, or did not otherwise comply with company protocol. So, do not do this for class.

IF YOU DO THE WORK YOU SHOULD EARN AN A

False. An A represents superior work. If you do what your teacher asks and complete all the material for a course in a satisfactory fashion then you should earn a C. If you do a good job with the material you should earn a B. Just because you complete your assignments based on their requirements does not mean you should earn an A for your work. Understand that A's are reserved for demonstrated mastery of the course material. If you have any questions as to what type of work will earn you an A just talk to your professors or consult your university's grading policy. It is amazing what people will tell you if you simply ask them.

Here is the breakdown of the grades at a state institution where a friend of mine works (Bloomsburg University of Pennsylvania[7]):

A = Superior attainment
B = Above average attainment
C = Average attainment
D = Minimal attainment
F = Failure

And here is a policy from a major research university (University of California, Los Angeles[8]):

A = *Superior*
B = *Good*
C = *Fair*
D = *Poor*
F = *Fail*

Here is the policy from a private university (St. Edward's University[9]):

A = *Excellent*
B = *Good*
C = *Average*
D = *Passing, but usually not transferable*
F = *Failure*

And here is my favorite explanation of grades (from California State University, Long Beach, where I currently teach[10]):

A = *Performance of the student has been at the highest level, showing sustained excellence in meeting all course requirements and exhibiting an unusual degree of intellectual initiative.*
B = *Performance of the student has been at a high level, showing consistent and effective achievement in meeting course requirements.*

$C = $ *Performance of the student has been at an adequate level, meeting the basic requirements of the course.*

$D = $ *Performance of the student has been less than adequate, meeting only the minimum course requirements.*

$F = $ *Performance of the student has been such that minimal course requirements have not been met.*

You get the point. All of these universities pretty much say the same thing. If you do truly excellent/superior work you will earn an A. If you do a good job you deserve a B. If you complete all the course requirements in a satisfactory manner you will earn a C. D's reflect minimal completion of course requirements and everything below that is considered failing.

Although you may think that you have done a good job in a class, before you tell someone that you deserve an A you have to ask yourself if you really did a *superior* job. Ask yourself what you did to go above and beyond the basic requirements of the course. And while looking at your grades be honest with yourself when you think about what you truly deserved based on your mastery of the material and the professional execution of your assignments. Sometimes you may not like your grades. But if you conduct a thorough and honest assessment of your work, you may realize that the grades you earned were deserved.

In the paragraph above, the reason for my saying that you have to make an "honest" assessment is because people have the tendency to believe that they do superior work when compared with others. This notion is tied to the concepts of selective perception and the self-serving bias. Selective perception suggests that people tend to interpret events based on their needs, wants, and expectations.[11] For example, people might tend to selectively remember the things they did well in class while forgetting the things they did not do so well. The self-serving bias suggests that people tend to have overly positive views of themselves.[12] For instance, ask a room of one hundred people how many of them consider themselves to be above-average drivers and you will notice that more than fifty people will raise their hands. Statistically speaking, this should not be the case.

Because people are biased and tend to perceive themselves as better than they really are, you cannot really trust them to make accurate assessments of themselves. Your professors, on the other hand, take a more objective approach to giving grades— it is our job to do so. We can see students' weaknesses and strengths in a more impartial manner than you can. Therefore, you need to trust your professors and remember that just because you think you did well on an assignment does not mean that you actually did.

Finally, although you may not always receive the grade you *want* in a class, realize that that doesn't mean you did not learn anything. Often it is better to learn a lot and get a C than it is to learn a little and get an A. Once you get out of college employers do not really care what your GPA was; what they care about is your ability to do a job well. In fact, one study, which looked at hiring personnel from some of the largest and most influential companies in the United States, found that scholastic achievement was ranked eleventh out of a possible thirteen variables used to judge potential employees[13] (see Chapter Six).

So, do not worry about your grades. Instead, worry about learning. You are going to get out of college one day and people are going to think that because you took a class in negotiation (for example) you can successfully negotiate with others. You will be embarrassed when you tell them you got an A in the class and then proceed to stare at them blankly, not knowing how to begin a bargaining agreement. Once you get out of college what matters is your expertise, not the letter you received on a report card.

PROFESSORS LIKE TO GIVE TESTS

This one is false too. In fact, giving tests means that your professors have to do a lot of work. Creating a test from scratch is difficult and it takes, literally, dozens of hours to do it well. In addition, once *you* are done with the test *we* have to grade it. This is not fun. There are a million things professors would rather be doing than grading tests including riding vintage motorcycles, feeding ducks, and reading big books through a monocle near a fireplace while sitting in a rocking chair and smoking out of a corncob pipe and touching a cat's face.

Cat resting after having its face touched.

Not only is making tests hard, but making them fair is even harder! Whereas one person likes multiple-choice tests, other students like short-answer exams. Still others prefer essay tests. Then maybe one person studied a lot and knows one chapter well while another student put more effort into another chapter. It is hard to make tests that are fair, that are challenging, and that please everybody who takes them.

Nonetheless, rest assured knowing that your professors have a multitude of tools to assess the fairness of their exams. For instance, with multiple-choice tests there are a variety of statistics that professors can use to figure out how good their test questions are. For example, professors can use item analyses to examine how many students picked the correct answer to a multiple-choice question and how many students picked the incorrect choices. Based on this information, professors can tell whether most of the students got the question right or wrong, and if the majority of students got the question wrong the statistics can tell professors if the students tended to all pick the same wrong answer. If this were the case it would indicate that perhaps there was a poorly written test question, or that the students were confused about the question (or the answer), or that the students simply did not study but all guessed the same answer. One way to figure out if the latter occurred is to look at who did well on the test and then examine whether these students tended to miss the same question in the same way as did the majority of the class. Anyway, the moral of this paragraph is this: although tests will never be perfect, your professors try hard to make them fair and we have mechanisms to check their fairness.

OK, so if you don't want to take tests and if making them is so hard for us, you may be asking why professors give tests in the first place. You know why? Because tests are necessary. Tests do two things: they get people to read and study and they help demonstrate who has mastered the material in the course. In all of the classes I have ever taken it is clear that I remember the most from the ones I had tests in. Why? Because I was forced to read the material and learn it. I was forced to synthesize what I was exposed to in class with the knowledge I already had in my brain and that process helped me to learn and remember the material. I know for certain that many students who have professors who don't give tests do not even buy the textbook assigned for the class. This is testimony to the fact that tests are good at accomplishing the first goal mentioned above.

In addition to getting you to read and study, tests also help differentiate between students who know the material well and those who don't. I am sure that if you study for a test you will want to be rewarded for learning the material. And that is what tests do, they reward you for mastering the information presented in your courses—just like on Halloween when people reward you for dressing up. As such, think of tests as the Halloweens of your classes: they can be scary but they can also be fun.

IT IS YOUR PROFESSOR'S JOB TO KEEP YOU ON TRACK WITH YOUR WORK

Ha-ha-ha. Not even close! Professors expect you to take responsibility for your own work. Although professors are willing to help you, the first thing you need to do is help yourself. Step 1: Get a planner and keep your schedule organized. Do not rely on your ability to recall important dates, events, and deadlines. Your memory *will* fail you at some point. Step 2: Do your work and do it well. Keep up with your readings instead of letting them pile up. Take good, clear notes and ask questions when you are unsure about something. I have to repeat that because it is so important: *make sure you ask your professors questions when something is unclear.*

At the end of every semester I usually have a student or two tell me that they wished they had more direction on a certain assignment. This is the case despite the fact that a) my assignment requirements are clearly articulated in my syllabus and b) I always take class time to talk about my assignments and ask if there are any questions. Unfortunately most students do not ask questions. Even fewer students come to see me during my office hours and ask for information. If you are unsure about something regarding your education then you need to do what it takes to figure things out. Ultimately, you are the one responsible for knowing the material in class; professors cannot read your mind and tell if you understood things or not. Remember, although providing the structure for an education is your professor's job, learning is yours.

YOU ARE TOO BUSY TO DO ALL OF YOUR SCHOOLWORK

I know this one is definitely false. I was a student once too. I used to tell people that I was *soooo* busy in college ... total baloney. I woke up at ten o'clock, took two-hour dinners with classmates, went to friends' dorm rooms to play video games, and had talks in the lounge for hours about random things like how long it would take a person to catch a squirrel if he or she were forced to try to catch one in a racquetball court, naked. An average full-time student probably spends about fifteen hours of his or her time in the classroom per week, leaving one hundred and fifty-three hours to do other things. Compared with high school, college is a vacation from class. The bottom line is this: you have time to complete your assignments. To do so you just have to do two things—manage a schedule and make sacrifices.

Let's first talk about managing a schedule. Although there are many texts available to help you learn about time management, I bet you have not—and will not—read them. So, let me give you some tips of my own. In my experience, time management really boils down to priorities. That is, in order to devote enough time to do anything you need to figure out what is most important to you and then you need to schedule less important tasks around that. Therefore, if school is your priority you need to make sure your work schedule, your social schedule, and your personal schedule all come second to your academic success. This means finding a balance between your extracurricular activities and your schoolwork.

Finding this balance is important. Take working while in school for example. I know that some of you have jobs that take up your time and I also know that working while in school can be important for a variety of reasons. That said, my advice to those of you who work is to examine the necessity of having a job while in college and then decide the best way for you to handle the demands of your work and the demands of your classes; there are limitations to how much you can expect from yourself. What that means is if you don't need a job then perhaps you should consider focusing on school and finishing your coursework in a timely fashion. Alternatively, if you *need* a job and you have one that, for instance, necessitates twenty hours of your time per week then consider taking a light class load so that you can balance your schedule and devote an appropriate amount of time to your studies. And if you have a job that requires forty hours of your time per week then consider taking some time off from school or taking just one class per semester so that you have the time you need to focus on your priorities. The same principle of balance should be applied whether you have a family, are sick and need medical attention, or have other important obligations. You need time to do your schoolwork, so set up your schedule to ensure that you can devote enough energy to your academic success.

OK, so let's say you figure out your course load for college and let's imagine that you have balanced your schoolwork with your extracurricular activities. The next part of managing a schedule is setting up your study routine in a way that maximizes your time for learning. To help you do this let me suggest three ideas. First, create chunks of time for yourself when you need to study. Instead of saying, "I will study tonight," actually set aside from six to ten in the evening as your designated study time. Set your day up so that you will have these hours free and do not schedule anything else during this time; you need to learn how to say "no" to others and to yourself when you need to study and something competes for your attention. Importantly, have these hours articulated and planned out. Make sure you are specific so that there is no question regarding when you should be studying and when you should be doing other things.

Second, make sure you study in a place that allows you to use your time wisely. If your dorm or apartment is distracting then go to the library. If you are tempted to check your phone when someone texts you then turn it off. Every time you become distracted by something in your environment you cheat yourself out of the time you set aside to learn. This means that either it will take you longer to study and that you will have less time for other things or that you will not study as much as you need to. I am sure you will agree that both results are suboptimal.

Third, to help manage your time, create to-do lists to help you organize your school activities in order from the most to the least important. These lists will help you keep track of what you need to accomplish and also help determine how efficient you are being with your time. I suggest that you make these lists on a daily basis. I also suggest that you put these lists on a daily calendar and set them up from week to week so that, as the days pass, you can see what you have done and what you have left to do. By creating lists for yourself you can organize your schedule and you will be able to check your progress when it comes to completing your tasks.

The information in the preceding paragraphs is helpful because my recommendations create a method for holding yourself accountable for your time. I know that it might seem weird to have to do this but, as is often the case in life, a lot of us need to create this type of structure for ourselves if we are to attain our goals. Studying for a class (or five classes) may seem like a daunting task if you look at it in its totality. But by creating daily, manageable chunks you *will* be able to get all of your work done.

Now that you know how to manage a schedule, let's talk about making sacrifices. In order to have time for your studies you will need to make some of these. This means that you will have to make choices about how you spend the hours of your day. To illustrate how this works let me tell you a story. One year I was teaching a class that required students to complete a group assignment. Although most people had no trouble making arrangements to do the project, I had several students from one group tell me that they had no time to meet their fellow classmates to complete the task. They told me they were "sooooo busy" and that they did not know what to do. Later that week I went to a fine dining establishment to get a refreshing beverage to quench my thirst and who showed up at the bar but all of the students in the group (separately). I about died laughing and spit up my nonalcoholic cocktail in both surprise and disgust. Do not tell me that you have no time to meet in your groups and then all show up to a bar at ten o'clock. If you are all at the bar at that time I am going to assume that ten is a good time to meet for you all. It might not be ideal, but that's OK. There will be plenty of time for you to go to bars in college.

What I am trying to illustrate with this example is that you need to think about what really matters to you while in college. If it is going to bars then you may agree that what my students did was a good move. On the other hand, if what matters to you is doing well in your classes and going on to a successful career then this may not be the case. You may truly think that you have no time to do all of the things you need to do for class, but if you take a hard look at your schedule I am sure you will find this to be an exaggeration. Wake up an hour earlier, take less time during meals, don't waste time on Facebook, lift weights for shorter periods of time, or forgo one party a week. If you take a realistic look at your schedule you will see that twenty-four hours in a day really is a long time if you can manage it well and make the right choices when it comes to doing what it takes to succeed in school.

Let me conclude by saying that I know that people have lives outside of class and I know that they have things to do in addition to studying. This is always going to be the case. My advice: just don't let those other things get in the way of your schoolwork. According to researchers, if you want to function effectively as an adult you need to learn future-oriented self-control.[14] That means delaying your gratifications and putting off immediate pleasures for the sake of long-term goals. If you decide that you want school to come first then you need to dedicate yourself to this goal and do what it takes to make sure you achieve it. This may not always be easy but if you want to do well in college you have to be prepared to make some choices. Take a step back in your life, assess your aspirations for college and your career, and make decisions that help you reach your objectives. This may mean that you have to change the way you prioritize your life but, trust me, your future self will thank you.

ALL PROFESSORS ARE GOOD

Although I wish this were true, sadly it is not. Unfortunately, most professors are never offered the opportunity to learn what it takes to teach well. While a plethora of research can be found in the field of instructional communication, many of the people teaching at universities have never even heard of the discipline. Teaching well at the university level is difficult. Among other things college teachers have to be charismatic, they have to be likeable, they have to be able to stimulate and entertain students, and at the same time they have to be challenging.[15] Additionally, as professors, we have to make sure we are not incompetent in our subject (e.g., we have to know the content of our courses, give fair tests, etc.), lazy with our students (e.g., we have to grade papers on time, remember test dates, etc.), or offensive to others.[16]

Of course, many of the professors you encounter will be great teachers. But when you come across a professor who isn't, there are a few things you can do to help the situation. The first thing to do is adjust your attitude. Try to remember that although the professor may not be perfectly suited to meet all of your educational needs, it is still up to you to learn. For example, even if you think that a professor is boring you need to stay motivated in class. What that means is when you are in a "boring" class, quit looking at the clock every five minutes and find a way to pay more attention. Even though you may not high-five your professor at the end of each class period and thank him or her for blowing your mind, you are responsible for being an active participant in your education. As such, it is up to you, and you alone, to find the motivation to enable your learning.

The second thing you need to do when you have a difficult time learning from an instructor is help the teacher help you. If your professor is unclear or speaks too fast, ask him or her to repeat the information or slow down. If your professor is unorganized, consider asking for PowerPoint slides to accompany the lectures. I know that it may seem strange to offer advice to your professors, but if done in the right way it may help them as much as it helps you. Therefore, instead of waiting until the end of the semester to fill out a course evaluation with your suggestions, consider meeting with your professor one-on-one to address your concerns. However, when you do so, frame the situation wisely. Don't be a weirdo and just come out and say that you think your professor is a bad teacher. Instead, frame your message around having him or her help you. Most teachers I know are willing to look into student comments. And if professors believe they can help you learn more by adjusting the way they do things, I am confident that many of them will be happy to make the change.

The third thing you need to do is learn to adapt your behaviors to the relationships you have with your various professors. If one of your professors is terrible at answering e-mails, for example, then visit him or her during office hours to get help. If the professor is always busy with other students, then ask for a personal appointment. Just like students, professors are all different. And if you want to communicate with them in an effective manner, you may have to adapt your preferred method of interaction to suit the relationship.

Finally, though it may not always be an option, if you have a hard time learning from a professor, consider changing to a different one. To be sure, you will not always have the option of switching professors if you are unhappy with them. But if you discover that you have choices, I suggest you take the time to match your professors to your learning style—whatever that might be. If you need professors who are energetic and ask for class participation, then seek them out. Alternatively, if you prefer professors who lecture directly from the book and publish their PowerPoint slides online, find those professors. Matching your learning style with professors who can help you learn at your best may take a little bit of research, but doing so will help you get more out of your classes.

SO WHAT?

Hopefully, the information I provided in this chapter has helped you see college through the eyes of your professors and hopefully it has also helped you think about school differently than you have in the past. Although I covered the myths that I thought were most pertinent to your educational experience, I am sure that I have missed a few. However, with any luck you have already learned that for every experience there are multiple perspectives. For those myths that I have forgotten I encourage you to engage in perspective taking. Examine the situation from the standpoint of your professors and try to see how things could be perceived in a different light. Ultimately, the notion of understanding others is part of what it means to be an adult.

CHAPTER TWO

BE AN ADULT

BE AN ADULT

2

I know that at times you may not feel like you are an adult, but your professors consider you to be one and they hope that you act like one. Follow the advice in this chapter to discover what professors expect from you in college based on your newly discovered and special adult status.

One of the most important things to know when you walk into your college classrooms is that your professors consider you to be professional, adult students. They expect you to put school first and approach your studies in a mature fashion. That's right, in addition to class you may have a job, you may have a family, and you may have a significant other ... but for your professors these other considerations are just that, other considerations.

Remember, while college might seem like a fun and exciting four-year buffer between high school and a full-time job, the reality is that college is the first step in your lifelong career. Therefore, your job in college is to be a professional student and you should approach your studies in the same way that professionals approach their careers. You are among the lucky ones, you are not working in a coal mine for a living, you are not fishing for crabmeat on the show *Deadliest Catch*, and you are not at Wal-Mart greeting old people as they walk/hobble into the store. No, you are in college and this job is a lot better than the alternatives presented above.

Unfortunately, most students do not think of school as a first step in their careers and instead they think of it as a four-year social event. They think of it as a time to hang out, have fun, go to parties, and then post pictures of themselves on Facebook doing keg stands while drunk dudes cheer them on. Sure, all of these things are fun and, as a matter of fact, your professors know that your social experiences in college *are* valuable to you. However, the problems start when students begin to prioritize their fun ahead of their educations. Most professors don't really care about your specific social events outside of class and most will probably never know whether you do keg stands or not. But they will know if you come to class, they will know if you do your work, and they will know how well you complete your assignments.

Although professors are not worried about your extracurricular activities, they are concerned about whether you learn the material in their courses. And if you do not master the material, you will not earn a passing grade. So, since the government considers you to be an adult at age eighteen, I suggest that you do the same. The next few pages will outline how to do this. Being an adult in college means that you need to treat school like it is your full-time job. Specifically, this means that you need to show up to class, come to class on time, take responsibility for your actions, respect your professors, and master the basics.

SHOW UP TO CLASS!

Are you kidding me? Writing this in a book for adult students makes me feel terrible. Yet, I think many of you need the information. That or you need a kick in the pants. Maybe you need both. Studies consistently show that an important predictor of success for college students is classroom attendance.[17] No, Einstein did not conduct these studies. But despite their commonsensical advice, the idea of attending class eludes many college students. I can confidently say that the majority of students who do poorly in my courses are the ones who do not show up. They miss instructions for class, they miss class notes, they miss quizzes, they miss participation points, they miss opportunities to turn in assignments, and they miss face time with me, the professor. I do not understand why students do not come to class. I mean, I know that people understand cause-and-effect relationships: you punch a bear in the face and it's going to bite you. So I find it strange that people don't come to class but still expect to do well in school.

Now, don't get me wrong. On occasion a person is going to miss class. You may have a medical emergency, you may have a friend who is getting married, or the surf may be up. However, if you miss class, the reason for missing it should be a good one and you should understand your professor's policies when it comes to making it up. That is, some excuses will be OK and will allow you to make up assignments and others will not.

If you decide to miss class for something fun (e.g., the surf's up, it is national dog bite prevention week, a homeless man pays you to play catch in the park) then it is up to you to be an adult and simply live with your decision. Do not ask for an extension of a deadline, do not ask for participation points to be made up, and do not ask for any special favors. Part of being an adult means that you take responsibility for your behaviors and that you accept the consequences of your actions. If that means missing a five-point quiz because the surf was up then great, I hope it was worth it. If it wasn't, then don't go surfing during class.

For absences that are excused (check your university's policies regarding what types of excuses allow for class content to be made up) be sure to make the process of making up the work easy for you and your professors. That is, bring them the necessary paperwork if the reason for your absence needs to be documented, be sure to stay in contact with your professors while you are gone, and be sure to send them an e-mail (at the very least) to let them know *ahead of time* (or as soon as possible) that you cannot make it to class.

In fact, letting your professors know that you cannot make it to class, ahead of time, is important despite the reason for missing class. So, do it when you are not going to be there. Now, you may be asking why it is important to let professors know that you cannot make class ahead of time. This is important for two reasons. First, when you cannot make it to class and you communicate this to your professors, they will make arrangements to accommodate your emergency. They can help you formulate a plan for turning in assignments and they can set up special appointments to take care of other things (such as tests and participation points) as well. Second, they will think of you as a thoughtful individual; you took the time to alert them of your impending absence and they will appreciate your consideration. However, if you simply do not show up to class you leave it up to your professor's imaginations to determine why you are not present. When no explanation is given, research suggests that there is a tendency for people to attribute the negative actions of others to stable, personal dispositions such as irresponsibility and selfishness.[18] On the other hand, if you can provide information that would discount these negative perceptions, your professors may be less likely to form them.[19] To do this you need to provide an appropriate explanation. To be appropriate, the explanation needs to be provided ahead of time.

Moreover, regardless of your reasons for missing a day, if you cannot make it to class it is still your responsibility to turn in your assignments on time and to get the day's material you missed *on your own*. At the very least, arrange for a classmate to turn in assignments that are due and arrange to get lecture notes from somebody else. I suggest that the first day you go to class you make a friend and have a buddy system for notes. If you miss a day then you can stay caught up and the same will be true if your friend needs the help. You may not know this but professors have lives too. In addition to working really hard as teachers we do a lot of writing and research. Furthermore, we are on a variety of committees (that help run the university) which require a lot of work. On top of that we also have social lives. The last thing we want to do when you miss class is spend our time lecturing twice or answering e-mails that ask, "Hey professor, what did I miss in class? Did we do anything important?" My response to messages like this is always the same: "Dear A**hole, figure it out. Love, Dad."

DO NOT COME TO CLASS LATE!

Let me ask you a question, what do you think would happen if you came late to work on multiple occasions? I am sure most of you know the answer to this one. If you do not, try showing up late to your job on a regular basis and report back to me with the results. Coming late to work is unprofessional and shows a lack of concern for your employer. If it becomes a habit your boss is going to think less of you and eventually you are going to be let go. The same process that happens at work happens in the classroom as well. That is, if you come to class late on multiple occasions your professors are going to think less of you and your tardiness will start to affect your grade.

Now, admittedly, things happen. I know that a person can't always help being late. But when it happens on multiple instances it starts to reflect negatively upon you. Think about it, do you love getting dressed for a night out and then waiting on your friends to finish getting ready? Do you enjoy arriving on time to an event and then waiting for others to show up? Do you like it when people tell you they will pick you up at seven o'clock and then show up at eight? I bet you find this behavior annoying and, although you would let it slide on the odd occasion, if these types of things happened on a regular basis you would start to get upset. You may not think that your tardiness affects the way your classes are run or that it shows disrespect to your professors, but the truth is it doesn't matter what you think. In fact, it doesn't matter what the truth is! People do not act based on the truth. Instead, they act based on their perceptions of the truth. And when you arrive to class late on multiple occasions you will be perceived as an uncaring individual. You do not want your professors to think that you do not care about their classes. When it comes to benefit of the doubt time (e.g., at the end of the semester when you are on the cusp of one grade or another), your professors will look at these types of things to help them make their decisions about your grade.

OK, so sometimes the bus comes late and I know that this can be a bummer for you ☹. But as far as I'm concerned, this shouldn't matter. I mean, why are you catching the latest bus possible anyway? My father is never late to work. You know why? Because he shows up every day at six in the morning. Sure, his work doesn't start until eight but he shows up early to guarantee that no matter what may go wrong on his commute he has time to take care of it before it comes time to clock in. And guess what? My dad is the director of a major research corporation in Northern California. He is the head honcho for a number of reasons and those include his responsibility, his attention to detail, and his dedication to doing things the right way.

Although this example is admittedly extreme, you should apply the same principle in your lives as well. If you are a student of mine, never tell me that you were late to class because your bus was late. My response is usually "so what?" I am not responsible for getting the bus on schedule and neither are you. But you *are* responsible for being to class on time. Accordingly, do not cut your timing so close that you depend on others for your success. You are better than that. Being on time is up to you, it is not up to Joe the bus driver. And while it may be Joe's fault that you are late, ultimately it is your problem.

The same is true for turning in assignments for class. You are sorely mistaken if you think that your professors care that your printer wasn't working or that the library's printers were on the fritz the morning that you were supposed to turn in an assignment. Instead of thinking that the problem is "sad" for you, your professors are more likely to be thinking, "Why are you printing your assignment at the last minute in the first place?" Remember Murphy's Law: if things can go wrong, they will. Take the time to make sure that all of your assignments are completed *at least* a few hours early and then print them so nothing goes awry. If something does, you will have time to correct the issue.

TAKE RESPONSIBILITY FOR YOUR EDUCATION

Some people have what scientists call an internal locus of control.[20] Generally speaking, these people believe they have the ability to influence the world around them. People with an internal locus of control believe that they have a say in their fates. Other people have an external locus of control and believe, for the most part, that the outside world affects their lives. This is what I call the "Uncle Rico Effect." You know what I'm talking about. In the movie *Napoleon Dynamite*, Uncle Rico was convinced that if Coach had only put him in the game during the fourth quarter they would have won the game and been state champs. Uncle Rico would have gone pro, he would have made millions, and he would have met his soul mate ... things would have been different! As a student you need to adopt an internal locus of control for your academic affairs. Adopting an internal locus of control will help you with your studies in at least two ways.

For one, if you did not do well on a test, instead of blaming the circumstances an internal locus of control will help you look at what *you* did (or did not do) to prepare for the test and discover why this may be the case. Doing this will allow you to correct the issue for your next exam. For instance, perhaps you did not study in a manner that helped you do well on the exam, perhaps you did not study long enough, or perhaps you simply did not understand the material. With an internal locus of control you will realize that these explanations are more likely an accurate reflection of your grade than is the professor's desire to "get you." Professors do not do the "No A's Dance" at the end of the semester, and contrary to the beliefs of some people they actually want you to do well in school. Therefore, when you do poorly on an exam, it is important to do some introspection to discover what happened. With an internal locus of control you will most likely discover that the best way to correct the problem for the next time is not to get your professor to stop being a jerk; instead, it may be to study both harder and smarter.

Second, an internal locus of control will help you create a positive impression with your professors. People develop expectations about the communication behavior of others based both on their relationships and on the context of their interactions.[21] And negative violations of these expectations often lead to negative results. For example, some of my own research points to the notion that people have expectations for companies following a failure.[22] One of these expectations is that companies take responsibility when things go wrong.[23] I discovered that because people expect businesses to take responsibility for their actions when there is a mistake, *not doing so* leads to negative impressions of the company. The same is true for students. Professors expect students to take responsibility for their own educations.

Therefore, if you fail to take responsibility for your education your professors are likely to ascribe negative qualities to you. An internal locus of control will help you to prevent this from occurring.

So how can you take responsibility for your actions? Easy, by realizing that in college it is up to you to learn. Understand that one of the fundamental differences between high school and college is that in college learning is self-directed. That means you should not need a professor to breathe down your neck to get you to learn the material. YOU need to keep up with the readings on the course schedules, YOU need to remember when assignments are due as they are stated on the syllabi, and YOU need to make sure that you learn the material in your courses. Professors simply expect you to do these things. Your professors are not going to call your parents or even contact you to let you know they are concerned if you do not show up for class, if you turn in low-quality work, or if you do poorly on an exam. Most of them are just going to assign you a failing grade. Believe it.

RESPECT YOUR PROFESSORS

Conflict occurs in a variety of relationships and at some point it is bound to occur between you and your professors as well. You may disagree with a course policy, you may have questions about a grade on an assignment, or you may need to change the date of an exam. In any case, you will eventually have conflict with your professors and when you do you need to handle it appropriately. Although the word "conflict" typically has a negative connotation, know that it is normal, it is to be expected in your relationships, and it may lead to positive outcomes.[24] Consequently, when interacting with others it's important to remember that conflict is not a bad thing. Instead, how you handle the conflict determines the positivity or negativity of the relational outcome.[25]

OK, if handling conflict is so important then you may be wondering how you can do it correctly. You can handle conflict well by doing three things: first, by bringing up conflict when it is important to you; second, by doing so at an appropriate time; and third, by working through conflict respectfully. Let's begin with the first idea. Do not avoid bringing up a topic to your professors if it is significant to you. Despite the fact that professors are very, very powerful, our powers do not include mind reading. Most professors I know are happy to work through problems with students. To do so, however, the problems must first come to our attention. Realize that professors are flexible people that are willing to listen to your point of view. Also, realize that most professors appreciate their students and want them to do well. With that in mind, instead of complaining to your fellow classmates when you have issues with your classes or with your professors, consider talking to your professors themselves. Most of them will be glad for the opportunity to rectify the situation. If you turn away from conflict you may never work out your problems, you may never be able to discover why things are the way they are, and ultimately your relationships with your professors may suffer.

Second, when you decide to bring up conflict, you need to do so appropriately. To help you remember this in the future I want you to memorize this simple rule: there is a time and place for everything. That said, some times and some places are better for discussing conflict than others. When you have conflict with your professors do not approach them at the beginning of class—when other students may be around and your professors are getting ready for their lectures. And do not approach them at the end of class—when they are scrambling to get to their next classroom. Instead, if you have any type of conflict, even if you just need to ask your professors for a special request, you need to make sure you bring up the issue with them when they can devote the appropriate resources to the problem (a good time may be during office hours).

You also need to make sure that you bring up the conflict in private. *In private.* The matter is between you and the professor and it should never involve the entire class. Now why should you bring up the matter in private? I'll tell you why. Research suggests that conflict in relationships is usually about one of four things: content, you may have conflict over a grade; relationships, you may have conflict over your role or status in a relationship; identities, you may have a conflict over how you are portrayed or thought of by others; and processes, you may have conflict over how your conflict is being handled.[26] When you bring up matters in front of other people you change the nature of the situation. Instead of being about the content only, you are likely to bring other conflict dimensions into the conversation. And if you change the nature of the conflict you may also unwittingly change the possibility of obtaining the outcome you are expecting.

Let me give you an example. Sometimes I have students who need to reschedule an exam for certain reasons (a content conflict). If they ask me in front of the class, I *have to* say no. I cannot be seen as playing favorites or bending the rules (this creates an identity conflict because it challenges the type of person that I said I was in class) and I do not want to do that. On the other hand, if I am asked in private to accommodate a student's schedule then I am going to be more willing to entertain the possibility of rescheduling the exam. Doing so only entails working out the logistics of meeting to administer the test and does not involve me re-negotiating my identity with the entire class.

In addition to bringing up conflict, and doing so at an appropriate time and in a private setting, the third way to handle conflict well when interacting with others is to make sure that you respect them and the way they see themselves. Why? Because our egos are intertwined with our basic human needs which include a) autonomy, b) relatedness, and c) competence[27] and a failure to help a person fulfill these needs may bring about self-protective mechanisms. As illustrated in the example above, these self-protective mechanisms may not have anything to do with the conflict at hand. And importantly, when others enact this type of behavior their actions may be detrimental to your final goal. You need to know that if you upset people based on the way you treat them, they are prone to fight you at any cost; not because they think they are right, but because they want you to be wrong. Therefore, in your interactions with others in general, and when you have conflict with your professors in specific, be sure to help people feel a) that they are free to do what they want, b) that they are liked, and c) that they are intelligent. By doing these things you may find that people react to you more fairly than if you had treated them otherwise.

Ultimately, I advise that when you have conflict with others, and expect any type of change, you bring the problem up to them. In addition, you need to bring up the conflict when they are in a position to deal with your concerns appropriately. Finally, when you bring up your conflict, you have to be careful not to upset people based on their identities, the way you frame the relationship, or the way you approach the conflict. People may not always remember the content of your conversations but they will always remember how you treated them and how you made them feel. The same is true for professors.

MASTER THE BASICS

Before I conclude this section I want to mention one last important component of being an adult at college. That is, you need to master the basics. In college, mastering the basics means knowing your professors' class policies, knowing your university's policies, and keeping information related to your studies organized. It may seem simple, but if you take the time to master the basics your life on campus will be a lot easier than if you do not.

To begin, let's talk about knowing your professors' policies. Knowing the policies means that when your professors pass out their syllabi on the first day of class you *actually* need to read them. Yes, this *is* important. Your professors use their syllabi to lay out their course guidelines and to let you know exactly what they expect from you throughout the semester. Reading your syllabi will help you figure out what you are getting yourself into and will also help you figure out what you need to do to be successful in your classes. Reading your syllabi is something that your professors assume you will do and it is your responsibility to make sure you understand the rules of your classes as designated by your teachers. Do it.

In addition to knowing your professors' policies, the second thing I want to talk about is knowing your university's policies. Knowing these is an important step toward your success on campus. For example, important policies include the process for adding and dropping courses, the time frame for withdrawing from a course without penalty, and the ability to retake classes without the first grade affecting your cumulative grade point average. Other important policies may include figuring out how to register for classes, when to register for classes, and what classes you need to take (and in what order) if you want to graduate in a certain period of time.

Determining these policies may simply be a matter of searching for information on your university's Web site. Alternatively, you may need to set up meetings with professors, department chairs, or deans to determine what is needed from you to succeed. In any case, make it a point to take the time to get to know the policies at your institution. I promise that doing so will save you some major headaches down the road.

The third thing I want to address concerning your knowledge of the basics is staying organized. What would happen if you went to the library to find a book and instead of having a catalog of books on different floors and shelves the library simply had all of its volumes stored in a gigantic pile in the middle of a poorly lit room? What would happen is that you would never go to the library again. Why would you go if you could never find anything you needed? Libraries can have the greatest books in the world but if you can't access them those books might as well not exist. Because going to a library and not finding what you need can be frustrating, librarians make sure that their collections are organized and easy to access. The same should be true of your personal information. Think about the feeling that accompanies losing important documents, and think about how you feel when you know that you have something you need but cannot find it. The feeling you get when something like this occurs is probably that of anxious frustration. You don't want that sort of negativity in your life. Being organized will help save you time and will also serve as a blessing for your professional well-being.

If you want to be organized then I suggest you start with your computer. Instead of having a million documents displayed all over your desktop, create appropriately labeled folders to keep your information segregated. For example, whenever you start a new semester in school you can create a folder (to do this simply right-click, select "new" and then "folder"; if you are working on a Mac, simply press control and click, then select "new folder") on your desktop labeled by the semester. Then, once you click on that folder and open it you can create new folders for every class you are taking. If you have five classes that means you will have five folders. Within each class folder you should create other folders that help organize your information even further. For instance, you can create a folder labeled "class documents" for the syllabus and course schedule, you can create a folder called "assignments" for the work you do throughout the semester, and you can create a folder called "notes" for the PowerPoint slides and notes you take in class. Once you are done with each semester you can create a master folder for the academic year and then drag and drop each semester into this space.

I know that when you first create a file and place it somewhere on your computer it seems as if you will always remember its name and location. However, this is just not the case. Weeks and even just days later you may be surprised to learn that when you log onto your computer to access a certain file you have a hard time doing so because you cannot find it. Because you do not want this to happen you need to take the time to create folders, place them consistently on your computer (e.g., on the desktop or on the C drive, etc.), and label them with enough information so that when you look for the files later you don't spend two hours searching for them without any luck.

In addition to your computer files, you also need to be organized with the physical components of your education. That is, you need to be sure that you have a system for cataloging your class notes, your graded assignments, and your completed tests. This is important should you ever need to use the information to help a friend study for the same course, help yourself in another course by accessing information you already learned, or help a teacher determine a final grade by having your exams ready in case there was a mistake in scoring. To be organized you need to create file folders just like you would on your computer. And you need to organize them in the same way. Create labeled folders of information that are segregated by topic so that when you store them you can put them in master folders, or hard-backed three-ring binders, that are labeled for easy access.

Being organized is part of what it means to be an adult and taking the time to have your work streamlined and easy to access will make you more efficient. Learning to create and use an organized system will help you beyond the classroom as well. When you are in the working world people will expect you to keep a variety of information on hand and they will want to keep detailed records of your work. If you are unorganized you will be in for a world of hurt when people ask you to retrieve something. This is a fact. So, practice now and reap the benefits of being an individual with a well-structured education.

SO WHAT?

There are many things that come with being an adult and I am positive that I did not cover all of them in this section. However, I did cover the notions of showing up to class, coming to class on time, taking responsibility for your education, respecting your professors, and mastering the basics. Despite the fact that I did not cover all of the situations in which acting like an adult will help you, if you keep the general idea in mind you can apply the rule in a variety of circumstances. So the next time you are in a situation and trying to figure out the proper behavior to employ, think about what an adult version of you would do and do that ;-). I am simply asking you to take responsibility for your actions. Although doing so might not necessarily be something you are used to, taking responsibility for your behaviors will help you tremendously in life. As you will learn in the next chapter, it will also help you in your communication with others.

CHAPTER THREE

COMMUNICATION

COMMUNICATION

3

The way you communicate with other people is a reflection of how you think of yourself and will be echoed in the way they treat you. Your communication with others will create your reality.

The way you communicate with your professors will have a profound effect on your relationships with them and will help define you as a good student, a bad student, or just a body in a classroom. Take the time to get to know your professors and be sure to follow the proper rules of decorum when you communicate with them.

To become a competent communicator you must communicate both effectively and appropriately.[28] Sadly, most students do neither. Below, you will discover some advice pertaining to professors' expectations for competent communication. First, I will discuss e-mail and then I will discuss making an impression through meetings during office hours.

E-MAIL

OK, I know you just got done Facebooking your best friend about whether you should super-poke the cute girl from your morning class and I know you love the computer. I do too. However, even though the computer allows easy access to, and facilitates communication with, a variety of people in your life that doesn't mean you should treat the messages you send on it as one and the same. In other words, although you are used to writing quick and dirty e-mails to people you know, you have to make sure that you are mindful of your communication when it comes to e-mailing your professors. Despite the fact that e-mail is relatively informal, your relationships with your professors are not.

If you were to run into a professor on campus and start a conversation, how would it go? I assume you would say hello, introduce yourself, and then probably begin a conversation. Once you were done what would you do? You would probably thank your professor for his or her time, give him or her a handshake, and then say goodbye. This is the type of formal interaction your professors hope to have with you and if you want them to be satisfied you have to meet these expectations.

If it seems as if the paragraph above is commonsensical then congratulations, you are not a half-wit! The problem, however, is that even though people understand how formal interactions work they forget to utilize this information when the medium or the context of their communication changes. Remember, just because you are sending messages to your professors via e-mail does not mean that you should let the format of the message change the way you communicate with them.

Let's continue with a few examples of the types of e-mails you should not send to your professors. I have received many e-mails from students that closely resemble this one:

```
Hey! Can we meet in your office tomorrow?
```

Notice that, among other things, this message lacks a salutation, any type of context for the message, and also a name. This is not how you would communicate with me in person so why send an e-mail like this? When I get messages like this one the first thing I think is, "Ummmm? What was that?" Then I respond by writing, "Tell me you aren't serious with that message." Next, I forward your e-mail to my professor buddies and this is what I write, "Yo, check out how ridiculous this student is." Then we all laugh at you and I kick my dog in disgust. Ha-ha, relax, I would never do that. I love dogs (sort of).

When you write to your professors you have to be sure that you follow the same protocol you would when speaking to them in person. So, address them by their proper title, introduce yourself, and then write your message using full sentences. When you are done, thank them for their time and sign your full name. Let me repeat that, *sign your name.* Research suggests that not signing your name is one of the most irritating things you can do when sending e-mails to your professors.[29] So, sign your stinkin' name. Do not expect your professors to be able to, or spend time trying to, figure out who you are by deciphering your ultra-cool e-mail address that reads: poopypants385@csulb.edu. (Oh, and by the way, this should go without saying but, if your e-mail address resembles the one in this example, change it to something more professional ... shame on you.)

Really, the advice here is to simply be polite and considerate. This is not hard to do if you are mindful of your behavior. I suggest that you try to be polite and considerate in all of your human interactions, not just in your e-mails with your professors. Try it: open doors for others; say "please," "thank you," and "no thank you"; help others feel good about themselves; don't force people to do things but instead politely ask for their help; apologize when you make a mistake or do something wrong; and show respect for others at all times. You may be surprised at how a little change in your behavior can have a big effect on your life.

Moving on. You also need to check your spelling to make sure that your messages are written in proper English. Professors do not want to see text-like abbreviations in your messages to them because, really, they do not care how cool u r.[30] As an example, check out an e-mail a colleague of mine *actually* received from a student:

```
hi there sir tomorrow should b the first day
in ur class sir and well I hadnt showed up
bcuz i kinda moved in last thursday like
into ur klass I had to move around sum
klasses but as far as reading wat am i sup-
posed to read bcuz my computer wnt let me
see a syllabus o ur tracs page kan u please
get bak to me? thank u
```

I am not joking. I wish I were joking. I am not joking. This is what my colleague wrote me when he shared this e-mail:

HOLY SH*T!!! This is for real. I've noticed this guy on the roster and wondered why he hasn't showed up. Tomorrow is the 4th class day. Read his email below. I'm very scared.

Ha-ha, how funny is that?! Don't be the guy who scares your professor because you cannot write an e-mail. My colleague actually took the time to write the student back to teach him how to write an appropriate e-mail. Hopefully, this also helps you. This is how my colleague suggested the e-mail should have been written using the student's own language:

Hello Darrin,

Tomorrow will be my first day in your class. I haven't been in class because I moved in last Thursday and I've been moving around some classes. Can you please let me know what I should be reading for class? Also, my computer won't download the syllabus on the TRACS page, can you please email it to me? Thank you.

Mike Jones (not the student's real name ;)

And this is how my colleague suggested the e-mail should have been written had the student taken the time to do it right:

Hello Professor Griffin,

Tomorrow will be my first day in class. I apologize for my absence but I have had some problems with my schedule and my living situation and I am just now in a place to attend your class. Again, my apologies. Although I know that I am behind, please know that I'm going to do what it takes to catch up with the readings and assignments. I visited the class Web site and was unable to successfully download the syllabus. When can I come to your office to get a copy and talk to you in person about how I can catch up? Thank you for your time and I look forward to meeting you.

Best regards,
Mike Jones

You see how it works? Imagine how you would feel if you were sent the original correspondence and contrast that feeling with the one you get after reading the e-mail just presented. I'm sure you will find that the two messages make you want to respond to the student differently. That's the point.

Let me give you some more advice. To avoid being put in a book regarding how not to e-mail be sure to write your formal messages in a manner that you would be proud to send in a physical letter as well. Importantly, this takes more than just running spell check before you hit "send." Spell check won't catch when you use the wrong word in a sentence—for example, "defiantly" instead of "definitely", "it's" instead of "its", and "your" instead of "you're"—and it does not help you create well-organized messages. It takes rereading your messages to ensure that you have expressed yourself properly, accurately, and gracefully.

I consider myself a decent writer and my secret to writing decently is the same secret good writers use to become good—they edit. Nobody ever really has a terrific first draft of a paper, or message, or whatever. Instead, it is some subsequent edition that is worthy of reading. If you want to be a good writer then you need to read over your words more than once to make sure that you are expressing yourself the way you intended. Consider having others help you in this process as well. Have trusted friends look at your e-mails to catch mistakes you might have missed and use them to gauge possible reactions to your messages. If you think this is going too far then at least consider putting your e-mails away for five minutes and then looking at them with a fresh pair of eyes before sending them. Only send your messages once you are convinced that they will be read and interpreted the way you meant to write them. Once they are gone there is no getting them back.

Worse than poorly written messages is when students send me empty e-mails with their assignments attached in hopes that I will look at their papers. These e-mails have no text in the subject lines or in the body of the messages whatsoever! No names either! Students who send me these messages want me to look at their papers and send them feedback without having to go through the trouble of actually learning from their mistakes. If you need help with your papers then *go see your professors*. These people are in their professions because they like helping students. But they will not do your work for you. Instead of sending your assignments over e-mail, take your papers to your professors during office hours so they can teach you how to improve. Most professors I know simply delete these e-mails.

In a related vein, sometimes students try to turn in assignments over e-mail because they cannot or do not want to come to class. However, you need to understand that turning in assignments via e-mail is *not* the same as turning in assignments in person. If your professors allow you to turn in assignments electronically then good for you, keep it up. But if this has not been negotiated between you and your professors then you need to do what it takes to turn your assignments in physically. This may mean that you have a friend turn them in for you or that you hand them in before the deadline (when you are in class). Whatever the case, you need to make sure that you do things the right way, not the easy way.

Another tip regarding e-mails is that it is important that you always end the interaction. What do I mean by that? When someone takes the time to write you an e-mail it is important to acknowledge that you received the correspondence. Make this a habit. Do not just ignore the e-mail and assume that the person is OK with that behavior. You know for a fact that people like to be acknowledged in face-to-face conversations so why would you ignore someone in an electronic conversation? Not responding when someone sends you a message might lead people to believe that their messages did not go through or that you are ignoring them. This may result in a bad outcome. For example, in the past I have written students with dates and times to meet because they asked me to set up appointments to go over their work with them. Sometimes, after writing the students, they failed to reply. These students assumed that the conversation was over and that they simply had to meet me at the designated time on the designated date. However, because I did not hear back from the students with a confirmation, I assumed that they were no longer interested in meeting and I did not show up. This is a classic example of mis-communication[31] and it can be resolved relatively easily. When a professor sends a message and sets an appointment with you, simply respond by saying hello, addressing the professor, saying that you will be there, saying thank you, then signing your name. I know it seems really hard and time consuming but your game of *Rock Band* can wait. So be sure to always end the interaction so that you can be seen as competent and appreciative.

Two last things about e-mails. First, be sure that you check your account at least once a day. Most people expect you to do so and their actions will reflect this. That is, if you do not respond to e-mails from people within one business day they are going to assume that you are ignoring them. If you are not ignoring a person for a strategic purpose then this will not lead to a positive outcome. To fix this problem simply check your account at least once a day and respond to your e-mails as you receive them—if you need time to get back to somebody then e-mail them saying so and be sure to follow up like you promised. Second, make sure that the e-mail account the school has on record for you is the same account you check. It is easy to have a variety of e-mail addresses. However, if you do, it is important that you have them organized and accessible.

If it feels like you are jumping through hoops to do what I mentioned in the section above (or the book in general) then I am sorry. But in college there is a right way to do things and there is a wrong way to do things. This system exists whether you know about it or not and it has been around since before you graduated from high school and went on your senior trip to Mazatlan. The sooner you figure out how college operates and the sooner you figure out ways to make your relationships with your professors work (reading this book helps) the better. So don't just do whatever you feel like when it comes to e-mail. Instead, recognize that the relationships you have with your professors require communication that is considerate, thoughtful, and professional.

GO TO OFFICE HOURS

I know some students who employ tutors to help them learn. They spend hundreds of dollars to hire a person to teach them a certain subject. If you asked me, I would tell you that this is a waste of money. When you are in college you are already paying tuition to learn from professors, who are most likely smarter than tutors. So, in my opinion, hiring an outside source is redundant. The solution to the problem of needing help with a subject outside of class is to go to your professors' office hours and get help from them.

It constantly amazes me that my students do not take advantage of my office hours. I have gone semesters without contact from students outside of class. Yet, students consistently get bad grades on assignments. At some point in your college career you will have a problem in a class, you will not understand an assignment completely, or you will need extra help with something school-related. It is at these times that you should see your professors for help. Use your professors as a resource. They are smart, successful, and willing to help you. Take advantage of them while you can.

Taking advantage of office hours will help you in both formal and informal ways. First, as a formal benefit, it will help you gain a better understanding of how your teachers do a variety of things in their courses, including giving tests and assigning grades. I have had many students ask me to help them understand what it takes to outline the material in their books for all of their classes. These students have also asked me to help them learn how their professors grade. Unfortunately, both of these subjects are highly personal for professors. That is, they differ greatly from person to person. Therefore, my best piece of advice concerning these topics is … you guessed it, go see your professors! While in office hours you can ask your professors to go over your textbooks with you; as an example, you can ask them to use a chapter to show you exactly what material he or she recommends that you study and learn. Perhaps your professors will tell you to memorize key points in the chapters or perhaps they will tell you to know the general ideas and be able to apply them in personal examples. Whatever. What you need to realize is that all of your professors are different and if you want to do well in their classes you need to speak with them to learn what they expect from you. This goes for reading your textbooks, knowing how your professors grade, and, really, anything else pertaining to your classes.

Second, seeing your professors during office hours will help you informally because doing so will help you create a network.

My students constantly ask me what networking means and, because they know that networking is an important part of being a professional, they want to know how to do it well. Networking means that you cultivate a set of people who like and respect you both socially and professionally. Therefore, to create a network you simply need to meet people and develop positive relationships with them. In other words, when you meet people you have to treat them with respect and then keep the relationship alive by creating opportunities for positive interactions.

Keeping relationships alive is the key to networking and there are several ways to do this. For example, you can get together with people for lunch to ask them questions, you can send people e-mails with information you think they might use or enjoy, and you can invite people to important events in your life. To keep your relationships strong with your professors you need to go to their office hours. Get to know your professors as people, be relaxed around them, and let us help you. Ask us questions about the subjects we have expertise in, or consider talking to us to learn more about certain majors, possible job opportunities for a person in your field, or about some of our research if it interests you. Professors enjoy being around students and when you come in to talk, or even to simply visit and ask a few questions, you get some important face time with us. This helps you immensely. When professors get to know you, they become invested in your education and, as a result, are more willing to work with you. Although you and your professors have roles to fill, realize that professors are people just like you. And the more they get to see you and know you, the more they may end up liking you.[32]

I often hear students tell me that they think a network consists of a bunch of people you know. That is wrong. In reality, a network consists of a group of people who *know you*. Therefore, going to see your professors will help you network because by meeting them in their offices they will get an opportunity to do just that. And when it comes time to exercise your network, say by asking for a letter of recommendation or by asking for a job reference, you will be in a position to benefit from the relationship you took the time to cultivate. Understand that with your professors you can either be the student who sits in the back wearing the baseball cap or you can be Joe Chang. It is never a bad thing to have your professors know your name.

SO WHAT?

There are a variety of things to know when communicating with your professors. In this chapter we went over some ideas related to two contexts in particular, e-mails and office hours. The big thing to remember from this chapter is that when you interact with your professors you need to be mindful of your behavior. Instead of treating us like you would treat any other person, understand that we have a special relationship. Recognizing your role in human interactions is crucial in life, and by recognizing your role in healthy relationships with your professors you will be in a better position to navigate your interactions with us successfully. As we move on you'll notice that when it comes to being a great listener, recognizing your role in this process is crucial as well.

CHAPTER FOUR

LISTENING IN CLASS

LISTENING IN CLASS

4

Listening as a skill can be hard to do. But experience should tell you that anything in life worth having is hard to get. (If your experience didn't tell you that, I just did ... Booya!)

You know that when you walk into your college classrooms you are there to learn. However, you might not know that if you lack the skills needed to listen effectively you will never maximize your potential in the classroom. This chapter was written to help you understand what it takes to learn while in class. And no, just showing up isn't enough *insert frownie face*. Although many people think that listening simply involves sound entering their giant heads, they are wrong. In fact, there are six interrelated steps to listening as a skill and hearing sound is only the first step. There are five more that follow. I am going to tell you about them now!

As I just mentioned, the first step to listening as a skill is for a person to actually hear the sound that another person, or thing, is making. In addition, you must be able to see what people are doing in order to interpret their nonverbal communication. What I am talking about here is the simple ability to process information. So, the first step in listening as a skill is hearing or seeing. How can you use this information to help you in class? Simple, if you cannot see what is being written on the board, move closer. And if you cannot hear the lecture then you need to make arrangements to change this. For instance, when I was a student I sat in many classes where the professors left the door open. Often, other students would roam the halls and sometimes they would talk on their phones. When I was in class I was there to learn, and if I heard Jack talking on his phone about how Jill was a nasty girlfriend then I always took it upon myself to ask my professors if they minded if I closed the door. You should do the same. Try to cut out all physical distractions from your learning environment and concentrate on making listening easy. If there is someone next to you who is talking then either move or ask that person to be quiet. If the person refuses then simply ask yourself, "What would Chuck Norris do?" You know what he would do? He would roundhouse kick their hearts out of their chests.

The second step in the process of listening as a skill is to attend to the sound. This means to pay attention to it. Often, sounds can become background noise that gets filtered out of our conscious experience (such as traffic or a clock ticking). If you have ever slept with the fan on and forgotten that it is making a sound when you are in the room with it then you know that without attending to a noise you will simply not listen to it. Accordingly, if you want to actually listen to a sound you have to focus your attention on it. The same thing is true in class. Although you will undoubtedly take interesting courses while in college, it is quite possible that you will still want to daydream when your professors are talking. In fact, it is quite easy to do this (more on that later). But what you need to do is catch yourself when daydreaming, focus on the lecture, and make sure you are paying attention to your professors when they are speaking. A major barrier to listening is a lack of motivation. Therefore, you need to take an active approach to listening if you want to do it well.

The third step to listening as a skill is understanding. If you are talking to a person who is speaking Spanish, for example, you will have a hard time understanding him or her if you cannot speak the language. If that person said to you, "Yo quiero tocar su pajaro," you would never know that the speaker wanted to touch your bird. To come to this conclusion you would have to ask the person to speak in English so that you might understand what is being said. The same goes for class—while listening to your professors speak it is important that you make sure you can follow the organization and the logic of their lectures. If you cannot, then you need to raise your hand and ask them to clarify. People often think that what they have said inherently makes sense to their listeners. Therefore, without the appropriate feedback your professors will never know that you are having a problem understanding the material.

The fourth step to listening as a skill is remembering. That is, you need to remember the material presented to you if you want to count it as listening. If I were Superman my kryptonite would be remembering people's names. Five minutes after meeting somebody for the first time I cannot, for the life of me, remember his or her name. Although I hear the name, I never remember it, and many people would suggest that I simply did not listen when the person introduced himself or herself to me. The same is true of lectures. If you cannot recall what your professor said then either a) you did not listen or b) you might as well not have listened.

Here's a trick I use to remember names: every time a person tells me their name, I quickly think of a person who has the same name. Then I match the new person to the old person in my mind. This association helps me recall a mental picture of the old person when I meet the new person on a different occasion. And though I have a hard time remembering new friends' names, I am pretty good at remembering old friends' names. By using this method I have become better at remembering people's names. A similar trick that people use to remember lectures is to paraphrase the material. Try it. In essence, when you hear information in your lectures simply try to repeat it back to yourself in your own words. If you can do this you may be more likely to remember the content because you will have learned it in a fashion that makes sense to you.

The fifth step in listening as a skill is evaluating. This involves putting the material you listened to into a framework that you are already familiar with. Scholars assert that we have schemas that help us organize data in our brains. Schemas are like filing cabinets that hold information according to various categories. For example, you have animal schemas that help you make sense of the animal world. The facts that a cat is furry, sweet, loving, and cute all involve your cat schema. If you can evaluate new information and place it into a schema with other information that you are already familiar with (in other words, if you can think about how examples from your lectures apply to experiences from your life), you may be more likely to recall the new information in the future.[33]

The sixth and last step in listening as a skill is responding. This means that to be considered a good listener you have to provide appropriate feedback (both verbal and nonverbal) to the person speaking. Although responding to someone makes perfect sense in the case of a conversation, students often forget to do this while in the classroom. If you ever have the chance to look at yourself while listening in a college classroom be sure to e-mail me and tell me what you observe. I can place a pretty safe bet that you are simply sitting in a chair, you are probably slouched, have your hands folded in front of you, and your face wears a blank expression that mumbles "blah … teach me." You have to realize that this type of behavior is a big turn-off for professors. When the energy in a classroom is low professors get down. You have the ability to fix that with the way you respond to us when you are listening in class. More on this next.

A TRANSACTIONAL MODEL OF HUMAN COMMUNICATION

If you asked me to draw a transactional model of human communication, the transactional model of communication would probably look something like this:

Now, I know you are wondering why I would draw a transactional model of human communication. You are probably also wondering how many times I can write the term "transactional model of human communication" in one paragraph. The answer to the latter question is four. The answer to the former question is that you may learn a little bit about your role as an effective listener by examining how the communication process works. Although there are a variety of things we could discuss with this model, in the pages that follow I am going to talk about three ideas in particular. These ideas include feedback, barriers to listening, and the problem with human communication.

What you might notice first about the transactional model of communication is that it includes lines going from one speaker to the other. These lines indicate that both people in the conversation are sending and receiving messages at the same time. This is called a feedback loop. The presence of feedback implies that, instead of being a passive listener when interacting with others, you are constantly communicating to the person you are speaking with. This should make sense in a conversation when you are taking turns talking back and forth, but it also applies when you are simply listening. This is because when you listen to people, even though you may not be saying anything explicitly through words, your nonverbal communication (e.g., your posture, eye contact, head nods, etc.) can convey a lot of meaning. You need to be aware of this fact so that when you communicate with others you only send messages you intend to. You also need to be aware of this fact because nonverbal communication is highly reciprocal. In other words, when one person does something in an interaction (e.g., speaks loudly, moves forward, smiles more), the other person will tend to mirror that behavior.

Here's why this is key in communication. The way you listen to others affects the way they speak to you. If you understand this concept then you know that by providing appropriate feedback you can help speakers communicate better. Don't believe me? The next time you are on the phone with a friend try to read a book at the same time. What you will notice is that your friend will have a hard time being expressive because your lack of attention to the conversation will indicate an inherent disinterest. If your conversational partner senses that you have become disinterested, he or she may start to feel unvalued and may likely terminate the conversation. So remember, you are constantly communicating with others when you are listening to them and this information influences their interactions with you. Therefore, it is important that you take responsibility for your feedback and recognize your role in healthy communication interactions.

OK, I know that you will not always feel like being an active listener in class and I know that you might not always feel like sending expert feedback to your professors. But consider this, there is an idea in science called the facial feedback hypothesis[34] which argues that, because physiological processes can influence the way you experience events, the act of smiling can actually make you feel happier. I think the same thing may be true for listening. Therefore, even if you do not feel like listening in class, try to pretend that you are a good listener. Sit up straight in your seat, look the teacher in the eyes, give appropriate feedback with your facial expressions, and take notes at important points in the lecture. What you may find is that the more you try to listen in class, the more you actually pay attention. And importantly, by looking like a good listener and providing appropriate feedback, you may also help your professors lecture better!

Moving on. After noticing feedback, what you might spot next in the model of communication are the two barriers to listening (these are the lightning bolt looking thingies I drew). These barriers make it hard to pay attention to others because they compete for your attention and make the already difficult task of listening even harder. By being aware of what these barriers are, however, you may be able to take the appropriate measures to get rid of them and listen successfully.

The first type of barrier is physical noise. This barrier includes anything that will physically disrupt your ability to listen. As I mentioned earlier in the book, if you want to listen well you have to make sure you do what it takes to proactively remove physical barriers to your hearing and you have to put yourself in a position to be able to listen to the best of your ability.

The second barrier to listening is psychological noise. Psychological noise is anything that goes on in your noodle that prevents you from being able to listen to the material presented in class. In essence, psychological noise blocks you from consciously attending to the message. How does this happen? It can happen in a variety of ways. Maybe you have a test next period that you are nervous about. Instead of listening to the lecture at hand, you worry about the exam. Or, perhaps you just got in a fight with your significant other. Instead of listening to the lecture, you are thinking about all of the great arguments you should have made but couldn't think of in the moment.

Or, maybe psychological noise creeps up on you. It is a known fact that your brain can process more information in a minute than most people can speak in a minute. This means that, while listening, your brain has a lot of space left over to process other information. Unfortunately, instead of using this space to their advantage, most students allow their brains to distract them. It happens simple enough … while listening to a lecture you notice that your professor has on a blue tie. Then out of nowhere you think, "Wow that tie is nice, I wonder where he bought it. Speaking of buying stuff, I need to buy a new shirt for the party this weekend. It is going to be an awesome party. Maybe if I buy a new shirt I can impress all of my new friends and they will see that I am a great guy and they will give me the duty, *nay* the honor, of being the party DJ. With my new shirt on I will play the heck out of Sisqo's "Thong Song" and I will spin only the finest in hip hop dance beats. Still this honor will be a blessing and a curse, for while I can play whatever songs I want, I will be stuck behind the turntables. Not a great spot to be if I cannot meet new people," blah, blah, blah ... By the time you catch yourself in mid-thought you realize that you are thinking about nonsense when you should be listening to the professor. Not good.

The key to overcoming psychological noise in class is to notice when you stop listening to the lectures and actively refocus on the message. If you find yourself thinking about the test you have next period, or about how your significant other is a jerk, or about how you can't wait to dance to a song about thongs then you need to adjust your attention to fit the situation—you need to actively monitor the content of your thoughts and focus on the information being presented in class. And, if you are smart, instead of using the difference between a person's rate of speech and your rate of thinking to daydream about foolishness, you can use your brain's extra computing power to paraphrase the content of the lecture and think about how the material fits with other experiences you have had in your life.

The last thing I want you to notice about the transactional model of communication is that it is inherently flawed. I know, yikes! The problem is that in order to communicate the thoughts that are in our heads to other people we need to use symbols (i.e. words). Essentially, because you cannot throw the thoughts from your mind into the head of another person, you need to communicate using sounds (that can be transferred between people). One of the things you need to know about symbols is that they are not fundamentally tied to the objects they represent. Instead, they are arbitrary means of conveying a message to another person. That is, the word "cat" is simply a sound that we have agreed on to represent a fluffy, furry, lovable animal in our minds. We could have just as easily called a cat a "gato" (Spanish), a "chat" (French), or a "blortute" (my fun, make-believe language). As long as we all agree that a certain sound or word represents the animal, we can communicate.

The problem with this method of communication is that, unlike shooting an arrow into your head, I cannot shoot my meaning of a cat into your head. Instead, all I can do is hope to say a word that triggers a reaction for you. Here's the dilemma: because we have all had different experiences of cats, we are all going to think of different ones when I say the word. Don't believe me? Try it. Close your eyes and think of a cat. Got it? Think about what it looks like, what color it is, how big it is, what is it doing, and perhaps what you are doing to it. OK, ready? What did your cat look like? Was it a medium-sized cat with orange and gray fur and a big white chest? Was it sitting on a bench in Istanbul's Topkapi Palace with its eyes closed? Did it have white feet and skinny legs? Did it have really long whiskers? No? Well, what the heck? I wanted to communicate my thoughts about a cat to you so what happened?

What happened was that when you thought of a cat you probably thought of one based on an experience you have had with a cat. And, because we have all lived different lives, we have all had different experiences. What that means is that I can never communicate to you exactly what I mean by a "cat." Sure, I can communicate generally, but I can never hope to get you to think of a cat in the exact same way as I do. We can get close, but communication between people may never be perfect. Not only is your image of a cat likely to be different than mine, but your feelings about cats are sure to differ too—adding an extra problem to our potential for miscommunication. And think about this: if we cannot communicate clearly about a simple, tangible object like a cat, what happens when we communicate about complicated things such as "love," or what it means to be "free," or what it means to be "good parent"? Depending on who you speak with the meanings of each of these words are bound to be different. Human communication is inherently flawed and to expect that what you said directly translated into what someone else heard is potentially disastrous. Do not do it. The same is true for you as a listener. Do not assume that what you heard is what a speaker meant to say.

All right, if the communication process is flawed then how can you fix it? By using more communication! Hooray! To communicate with somebody effectively it is important that you provide feedback to the person you are speaking with to verify that you are both on the same page. Using a feedback mechanism is the only way to ensure that what you think you heard is actually what the person talking meant to say. Therefore, instead of relying on a single message for the foundation of your meaning, I recommend that you create loops of interaction to help you communicate with precision. There are a few ways to do this.

One way to make certain that what you heard is an accurate reflection of what someone meant to say is to tell that person your interpretation of their message and then ask him or her to report back to you regarding whether your understanding is correct. For example, in the transactional model of communication I drew, the smiley face on the right is trying to verify with the other smiley face whether the cat he is thinking of is the same cat as the one being described. By doing this, the smiley face on the right is trying to ensure that when he continues the conversation he and his conversational partner are talking about the same creature.

A second way to make sure that what you heard is an accurate reflection of what someone else meant to say is to ask for more information. For example, if a man is speaking to you and you think you hear him say he does not like your cooking (e.g., maybe he says "this pasta sauce tastes different") you may want to double-check his meaning by asking him what he meant by the word "different." You may discover that what you think he said was not his intention after all. That is, though he liked it, perhaps he was not expecting to taste a sweet and spicy sauce. Take a moment to think about how much trouble using feedback can save you in your personal life.

Take a moment to think about how much trouble using feedback can save you in your studies as well. Many of my students listen to my lectures and then simply assume that their notes are accurate and that they understand the theories we have discussed. Yet, when I ask for examples in class I sometimes discover that a few people have not understood all of the theories in the way that I meant to describe them. This is a problem of communication that I try to rectify by asking students to repeat the theories back to me using their personal experiences so I can check whether they are learning the information I have presented in the way that I intended. Although this tactic helps, many of your teachers will not do this. And even if they do, they might not ask you to personally repeat the theories back to them. Therefore, you need to make it a point to talk with your professors to ensure that you understand the ideas in their classes the way they intended for you to learn them. This is your job. Instead of relying on a single message to inform your education, you need to interact with your professors using loops of communication to make sure that what you are learning is accurate. I have had many students who thought they knew the information in my classes before a test only to find out from their low grade on an exam that, in fact, they did not know the content either fully or correctly. Don't be that person.

Did you think of this cat?

SO WHAT?

Listening as a skill contains six steps: hearing, attending, understanding, remembering, evaluating, and responding. However, because of the inherent flaws in communication, listening can be difficult. Still, despite the fact that listening is hard, I am positive that with work you can all (to quote the rapper LL Cool J) do it, and do it, and do it well. Just remember, this will take effort—to listen well you will have to be motivated to do it and you will need to be an active participant in the process.

The better you get at listening the better you will be at recalling information and using it down the road (for example, on tests). In addition, by listening correctly you will help create the healthy learning atmosphere that your professors require to lecture well. However, even though listening well is an important component of your education, it won't help you master your coursework by itself. To do that you also need to study. We turn to that concept next.

CHAPTER FIVE

STUDYING FOR EXAMS

STUDYING FOR EXAMS 5

Studying for exams take a lot of work. It is difficult to do well and takes a lot of self-discipline. Still, I know you and you can do it.

A large percentage of the students I teach seem to have a hard time understanding the correct method for studying. I think this is normal. Just like a lot of my students, when I first got to college I had no idea what to expect from my tests. Correspondingly, I also remember being clueless about how to study for them. I eventually discovered what it took to do well on my exams and the lessons I learned from my undergraduate experience were ones that I used throughout my academic career. And, now that I have field-tested my procedures for doing well on tests, I can confidently tell you that they work.

In this chapter I am going to do a few things. First, I am going to teach you a simple method for doing well on exams and I will outline the process you need to follow to make your dreams of getting A's on tests a reality. Then, after you learn the formula for doing well on exams, I will ask you to do *me* a favor and promise me two things ... you need to read on to discover what those are. Finally, I will conclude this chapter with a discussion about how you can be strategic with your exams so that you can study both harder and smarter. You are welcome.

THE FORMULA

There is a simple three-step formula for doing well on tests. I followed it, my students who earn A's follow it, and if you want to do well on your exams then you should follow it too. Because I like you, as a friend, I have decided to share the formula with you in this book. So, here's how to get A's on your exams:

First, get good information. That means read your assigned books, attend class lectures, and take good notes from both. It is of the utmost importance that you make sure the information you are trying to retain is both accurate and complete. But do not rush this process! Ask your professors questions if you have holes in your lecture notes and take your time when reading your textbooks. Taking the time to make sure you get good information is crucial and this means that you have to be strategic with the way you expose yourself to the material presented in your courses.

Sadly, a lot of students think that if they come to class and read the book one time they will perform well on their tests. This is simply not the case. After going to class and after reading the chapters you need to move on to the second step toward getting A's on your exams: studying and memorizing the material. Now, when I say "memorize" I mean that you actually have to learn and *know* the material in your courses. Shoot, a monkey could learn to recognize a term in a textbook, that's not the point of college.

Instead of merely studying to recognize terms on a test, try to integrate the information you are exposed to into your personal knowledge base. That means understanding concepts as they apply to your life and expanding on ideas in the book as they relate to your world of experience. Study so that you are able to provide real-world examples of the phenomena you are learning about and study so that you can apply the concepts you are exposed to in contexts other than the ones they are paired with in the text.

The third step to earning A's on your exams is to teach the material to somebody else. Practice presenting the material to others because, as is often the case, when you try to articulate your thoughts out loud you will quickly discover that the material you were sure you were familiar with is not as well memorized or as organized as you thought it was. When you reach the stage in your test preparation where you can create original examples based on the material you are studying and can teach the material to somebody else you will be in a good place for the exam. And guess what? This is what it means to learn and this is how your college experiences will help you once you are working in a professional environment. By actually learning a discipline—instead of trying to do well on an exam by simply memorizing terms—you will develop an area of expertise that will be marketable to future employers.

What you should take away from this section is that studying for tests is a good way for you to learn a body of knowledge that will be valuable to you in the future. So, with that said I want you to promise me two things. First, promise me that you will take your tests seriously and see them for what they are, a method designed to force you to learn. It may sound odd to put it that way but as I mentioned in the section on myths, if professors did away with tests I am confident that a lot of students would simply not read or study. I want you to see the utility of exams and I want you to learn to appreciate them instead of dreading them.

The second promise I want you to make me is that you will never ask your professors if what they are teaching "will be on the test." In reality, it shouldn't matter what's on the test. Exams act as a method to check that you learned the material in a given class through a selection of various items. Because tests cannot cover everything, your teachers use a sample of questions to verify whether you learned the material. The point of your taking an exam isn't that professors want you to know, say, fifty pieces of information on a fifty-item test. On the contrary, the point of taking a test is to demonstrate that you read, understood, and learned the material in the entire course (or section of a course). The number of questions that will be on your exams and the exact material on them shouldn't matter. Stop studying to get those answers right and start studying to do well on your tests no matter what you are asked.

BE STRATEGIC

When you study for your exams you have to be strategic in the way you prepare. Instead of doing what has worked in high school, try to study smarter. Three ways to be strategic in your approach involve reading your textbooks the right way, using the spacing effect to improve your memory, and studying in teams.

The first thing you need to be strategic about is how you read your textbooks. Know this: it is hard to read a textbook cover to cover like you can a novel. The information provided in textbooks is typically denser than what you find in novels and it is harder to digest in one sitting. This is especially true if it is the first time you are exposed to the material. So, do not try to read a chapter in one pass and then think that you are prepared for an exam. You are not. Instead, read a few pages at a time, take short mental breaks to process the information you learned, and revisit the chapters you read more than once. Reading the chapters slowly and doing so on multiple occasions will help you learn the information accurately and it will also help you memorize the information you are studying.

Next, you need to be strategic about memorizing the material. One thing you should know about committing information to memory is that anybody can do it. This is one part of school where hard work is very often associated with success. To commit something to memory does not take talent or intelligence, it just takes hard work, diligence, self-discipline, and repeated exposure to the information. To be successful do not try to memorize the day or even the weekend before an exam. Instead, I suggest that you start memorizing as you go. Researchers who study human memory acknowledge a "spacing effect"[35] that suggests the mind best stores data in long-term memory when it is exposed to information repeatedly at the point where you almost forget it. That is, long-term memory is best formed when you repeatedly expose yourself to information over longer periods of time as opposed to shorter periods. Therefore, my advice to you is, instead of cramming for your tests, read along with the weekly assignments and spend a few minutes/hours each night devoted to looking over that week's material and thinking about the concepts in a meaningful manner. This way you are more likely to commit the information you are learning to long-term memory. Trust me, this will work. Let me give you an example.

When I was an undergraduate I used to write my notes from my classes and from my textbooks in a spiral binder. I would integrate my lecture notes with the notes from my textbook so that I would have one coherent set of information. Then, every night before I went to bed I simply looked at the day's notes and read over them. Looking over the notes probably took about ten minutes per class. As the weeks progressed I would add material to the binder and would read it some more. I would not try to memorize the material. Instead, I tried to become familiar with it and think about it using examples from my life. Sure enough, when the time came for my exams I had very little to study. Because I had been reading the material for such a long time, I just sort of learned it. I did not study much the day before an exam and, in fact, these were the days when I was usually the least stressed. I knew I had the material down and I knew that there was little I could do to prepare in the short twenty-four hours before the test.

If you decide to cram for a test you will not do well. To master the material for an exam you need to divide your learning into manageable chunks. You cannot read and remember ten, five, or even three chapters if you sit down for one night and try to learn it all. You simply cannot intelligently process the amount of information you need to learn for a test in such a short period. To help you understand this point I want you to think about studying as being similar to a cross-country road trip. If you needed try to drive from Los Angeles to New York City in one week you could do it if you paced yourself and drove about four hundred miles a day (total distance is about 2,767 miles). But if you waited until the last minute you would never reach your destination. Just as it is physically impossible to make a forty-three hour road trip (according to Mapquest.com) in twenty-four hours, I am sure that you will find it impossible to master all of your course material by cramming the night before a test.

Finally, studying in teams is another great way to be strategic about the way you approach your exams. Think of this as a method of dividing and conquering your task at hand. If you have a ten-chapter test coming up, instead of trying to outline every chapter, consider getting a group of people together and splitting the workload. Although I always recommend that you read each chapter yourself, the process of outlining the material doesn't have to be a one-person job. If you create a group of five people and delegate two chapters per person you will be able to spend less time outlining and more time studying. Again, reading all of the chapters yourself is crucial. This is important to ensure that you understood the examples in the text and to make certain that you have interpreted the major ideas correctly. An outline is a condensed version of a chapter and it will only help you remember the material if you can figure out how it relates back to the bigger picture of the book. Therefore, my advice is to learn the material yourself, but use the help of others to streamline the process of studying for tests.

SO WHAT?

Doing well on exams is very tough but it is also very doable. However, if the statements I made regarding studying for tests seem too tiring or seem like they will interfere with your plans to do something this weekend then do not follow my advice. Just, when the time comes for you to review your test grades, do not be upset that you did not do well on your exams.

Something to always remember is that you are not entitled to anything in class or in life. The faster you learn to accept this fact the faster you will be able to successfully navigate your time on Earth. If you do not perform at your job you will be fired. If you do not earn enough money in your career you will not be able to buy groceries, or a car, or a house, or whatever it is you may want or need. Our nation was built by intelligent, pioneering individuals who worked hard to survive. They were not guaranteed houses, or jobs, or even survival, and neither are you. Our country was not founded on handouts for the lazy. No, we learned early in our nation's history that we are the masters of our own destinies. If you want to do the bare minimum to prepare for a test then do not expect to earn a good grade. Instead, accept your fate and wallow in the misery of being un-American.

Also wallow in the misery of being untrained in your course-work. Being untrained in your coursework means that you will be unprepared for your career. This is an important concept because you need to know that people will not pay you to perform a job just because you have a degree. Instead, they will pay you because you have some expertise that they do not have and that they need. Your diploma is a worthless piece of paper; it is the knowledge you gain from college that is valuable. That's why studying and doing well in your courses is such an important component of your future success. There are other important components as well. Read on and learn what else it takes to be successful in the next stages of your career.

CHAPTER SIX

THE BIG PICTURE—KNOW YOUR GOAL

THE BIG PICTURE— KNOW YOUR GOAL

6

You are in college for a reason. Figure out what it is.

Dr. Bolkan reached his goal of climbing to the top of a giant fallen tree. Be like him.

College is a place that will help you grow in a variety of ways. And, if you are like most people, you are going to get a lot out of your time in school. Although there are many things that college is good for, I assume that one of the things you would like to get out of the experience is a job. Because, presumably, you would like to be employed once you graduate, it is important that you understand what organizations look for in potential employees. This chapter was written to help you find direction in college so you can use the opportunity to put yourself in the best possible position for a successful future. In this chapter I will discuss two important aspects of your college experience: picking a major and preparing yourself for the workforce.

PICKING A MAJOR

Many students float around the halls of their universities without any direction. They have no idea what they want to do or what they want to be when they "grow up." This is too bad because although the decisions you are making now may seem inconsequential, in reality they are shaping the quality of your life to come.

One of the first things you need to focus on when you get to college is picking a major. Not only will doing so help you organize a schedule of classes and graduate on time, but picking a major will also help provide direction for your professional future. OK, so you know that picking a major is important, but how do you do it? There are a few ways to go about this. One way is to work backward. Simply figure out what you want to have in life and take an inventory of what you want your future to look like. I suggest that you be as specific as possible. Ask yourself questions such as, what kind of car do I want to drive? How big of a house do I need? What state do I want to live in? How many kids do I want to have? Do I want a boat? What types of jobs do I dread? Do cubicles give me the creeps? How many hours do I want to work per week? And, what sort of income do I want to take home? After answering all of these questions (and hopefully more) you may be in a better position to determine the types of jobs that will afford you the lifestyle you seek. Then figure out what majors are likely to lead to those jobs. One great way to do this is to talk to people who have the lifestyle you are interested in and ask them what majors they had when they were in school and what advice they may have for you as a student.

A second and related way to pick a major is to determine what types of jobs you would enjoy doing—without necessarily worrying about your desired lifestyle—and then figure out what degrees help lead to those careers. Although it may be a good start to talk with career counselors, I suggest you get a little more hands-on. Like I mentioned above, talk with people in the jobs you are fond of and ask them what steps they took to get there. Once you figure out what majors lead to certain career paths I suggest that you seek out seniors in the disciplines you are considering and ask them what they plan on doing with their degrees. Figure out where they are headed and decide whether their paths align with the future you have envisioned for yourself. You could also talk with alumni of the academic programs you are interested in and ask them where their careers started and where they have ended up. Doing this kind of research is important and the information you will get is invaluable. These people have done *exactly* what you are considering doing and their lives will be a testament to what you can do with your choices.

A third way to pick a major is to decide what classes interest you. Most universities allow you to survey a variety of courses before you pick a major. And even if you chose a major to begin your tenure at school, consider taking other classes to see what else is out there. When you find a course (or courses) that interests you so much that you would read the textbook or study the material on your own (i.e., even if you did not have the class) then think about making that class's discipline your major. Importantly, once you have an area of interest in mind look a little deeper and figure out what other classes belong to this field of study. Decide whether the discipline is one you can commit four years of your life to and try to determine if there are enough classes in the major to get you excited. Moreover, these classes should excite you both inside the classroom and beyond it. After all, you will spend an awful lot of time at your job, which will likely be related to your major, and it should be something that you are willing to dedicate a big chunk of your life to.

In reality, the best way to pick a major is to combine all of the aspects of the three methods of selecting a discipline outlined above. You will need to balance what you enjoy doing with what will afford you the lifestyle you want. Of course, those two things may be naturally aligned, but realize that this may not always be the case. Also, know that picking a major, if done correctly, should take a lot of work. This is good. This is important. Take your time and do your research. Picking your major should be done carefully because the choices you make now carry real-world consequences that will affect your life for many years to come.

WHAT EMPLOYERS WANT

Hopefully, you will follow my advice and do what it takes to pick an appropriate field of study. Still, even if you have a major and know what you want to do, you may not have a clue about what skills are sought after by organizations. This section was written in an attempt to enlighten you. After conducting several interviews with business professionals about what they look for when hiring new employees and after looking at the literature regarding what employers want from potential applicants, I noticed some reoccurring trends concerning important skills for college graduates. Specifically, employers are looking for well-rounded individuals who have soft skills (i.e., communication skills, leadership skills, etc.), hard skills (i.e., technical skills), and applied experience in the business world.

I want to go over soft skills first and we'll begin this section with the results of my interviews. The first few things the business people I spoke with told me that they look for in potential employees are good interpersonal skills. That is, employers are looking to hire people who can be successful at negotiating interpersonal relationships. When I asked for specifics, my interviewees said this means that you need to know how to handle conflict well, that you need to know principles of interpersonal influence, and that you need to know what attracts people to others. My interviewees also told me that they look for the ability to cooperate and work in teams and the ability of potential employees to lead others.

At this point many of you might think that you already have the interpersonal skills covered because you are outgoing. I bet that at least one person who reads this book will think that mastering interpersonal interactions is easy because he or she is a "people person." I have a PhD in a discipline that focuses on human interaction and I have to tell you that I don't even know what being a people person means. If you are extroverted, then great. But don't count on your bubbly personality to get you to the top of the professional world. Instead, you need to learn the skills necessary to help you navigate a variety of social and professional interactions. This means that you need to develop skills in interpersonal communication, small-group interaction, conflict management, persuasion, and public speaking, to name a few topics. To be an effective participant in your social and professional relationships you need to take classes in these areas so you can learn the skills that your various relationships require. These classes exist so find them (check in the Communication Studies department), take them, and smile knowing that you have just done something worthwhile for your future self. Then, instead of telling employers that you are a people person, you can tell them that you have developed the ability to successfully navigate interpersonal relationships in a variety of contexts. And, importantly, you will have examples to back up your claim.

Continuing with the soft skills, the business people I interviewed all said that they seek employees with good communication skills, both oral and written. This means that you have to learn how to effectively speak to others and that you have to become a good writer. Both of these skills are extremely difficult to master. What makes it worse is that we communicate on a daily basis and, as a result, people are not mindful of how bad they are at it. For example, a lot of people think that that because they speak on a regular basis they know what it means to speak well in a professional context. This is simply not the case. From my experience as a professor of communication and business consultant on the same topic I can tell you that *no* student or client has ever walked into my class a terrific communicator. All of them have needed to improve the content, delivery, and the organization of their messages. The same is likely true for you as well.

Many people do not write well either. This is a skill that almost anybody can master. Unfortunately, most people lack the desire and the self-discipline to do it. Sure, it takes a lot of work to become a good writer. But if you do it, you will be constantly rewarded for your skills. Instead of simply saying "I am not a good writer," take the time to learn the principles of writing well. Even though you may not become the next Shakespeare you can at least improve your writing so that you can communicate more effectively and efficiently. If you want a good reference for writing check out *Style: Toward Clarity and Grace* by Joseph Williams. This book has helped me in my career and I liked it because it was short, smart, and easy to read. Reading this book will take a few days but it will be a terrific investment in your future. In the meantime, if you need more immediate writing help, consider taking your papers to your campus writing center. This is a terrific resource provided by smart people who are waiting to help you at no cost. You would be wise to use the assistance.

Something that is upsetting to me as a professor is when my students tell me that they are not naturally good at a particular subject. This often happens when they talk about public speaking or writing. It's not that I don't appreciate that my students are trying to be open. It's just that I get upset with the idea that someone cannot naturally speak or write well because my students use it as an excuse to simply stop trying when they find learning these skills to be difficult. Off the top of my head I can only think of a few things that humans might be naturally good at. These include eating, sleeping, and perhaps running.[36] For almost everything else we learn to do things well.

If we only focused on doing what we were naturally good at we wouldn't be living in the twenty-first century as we know it. Do you think people are naturally good at operating motor vehicles? Should people be naturally good at programming computers? Is using a toilet something a person should be naturally good at? Depending on who you ask, the answer to all three of these questions may very well be "no." You want natural? Go live in a cave and eat raw toads for dinner like Bear Grylls. There will be times when school seems hard or when a certain subject seems like it is impossible to master; speaking and writing tend to be two of these subjects. However, instead of giving up, you need to believe in yourself and find the motivation to persevere. Instead of settling for mediocrity, take the time to reach your potential. You now know that speaking and writing are two of the skills that employers look for, so, even though they may be hard to master, make sure you do what it takes to develop these skills to the best of your ability.

OK, so you know that the professionals I interviewed think soft skills are important, but what does the research say? An examination of statistical data compiled by business professors and research institutions suggests that business owners and managers also want many of the skills mentioned above. For example, one study examined some of the largest and most influential companies in the United States[37] and sent surveys to the people listed as the heads of Human Resources in each company. Respondents were asked to rate the importance of various qualifications of potential recruits. The results presented on the next page list these qualifications from (1) most important to (13) least important:

1. Oral communication
2. Interpersonal skills
3. Leadership skills
4. Written communication
5. Decision-making ability
6. Analytical skills
7. Teamwork skills
8. Previous work experience
9. Financial skills
10. Technical skills
11. Scholastic achievement
12. Internship experience
13. Extracurricular activities

Another study examined data that reflected what more than 8,500 managers thought were important managerial competencies.[38] Results suggest that the top-rated competencies and skills were decision-making skills, human management skills (including skills related to organizational behavior, human resource management, leadership, etc.), and interpersonal skills.

Like the business people I interviewed, it should be clear that these studies also mention the so-called "soft skills" as being particularly important for professional success. In other words, most employers want people who are smart, motivated, and who can work well with others. These are skills that can be learned. Consequently, I suggest you commit to the idea of developing them.

Importantly, you need to remember that, in addition to soft skills, many employers are looking for hard skills and applied experience in a business setting as well. These things are important for would-be employers; the people I interviewed said they look for these qualifications and the list above cites them in items eight, nine, ten, and twelve. For some of these skills, you may be able to take classes to build your proficiency. For example, you can take a variety of math, business, and science classes that may help teach you the technical knowledge you need to know to perform a job. On the other hand, you may not always be able to count on school to help you develop skills you need to do well in a professional environment. And, more likely than not, applied experience can only come from working on a job or from your time working at an internship. Therefore, instead of simply relying on your classes to teach you about a subject and to get you employed, you need to get work experience as well.

Take a look at your résumé right now. Don't have one? Not cool. Create one and then look at it. I'll wait. OK, got one? Great. Most likely it is terrible. At this point in your life what information can you really hope to put on a résumé to attract potential employers? Right now the answer may very well be "nothing." And that is OK, *for now*. But, when you graduate from college, the same answer will be unacceptable. By taking the time to learn from a variety of sources and building your résumé with relevant experience (and no, working at the Olive Garden does not count as relevant experience) you will be in a good position to land a job once you get out of college. This notion is so important that it warrants repeating: if you want to improve your chances of getting a job when you get out of college then it is IMPERATIVE that you take the time to work in applied business settings and build your résumé with experiences relevant to your career goals. Some of the most successful people I know have used the professional experiences they got from internships and jobs while in college to help jump-start their careers. This is because when it came time to graduate they had a list of references and experiences they could draw upon to demonstrate their potential to employers. These people were smart and I will tell you that following their example is crucial to your getting a job.

Now, just how you go about doing this is going to be different depending on your current professional relationships, the types of internships/jobs you are interested in, and your geographic location. Because these variables will differ from person to person I will not spend much time here explaining how to secure applied experience in your field. Suffice it to say that the main thing you need to do is be proactive in your approach to getting these opportunities while in college. That is, you need to make it a point to get this experience on your own—no one is going to do it for you. Some places to start looking for internships/relevant jobs include corporate Web sites, your university's career center, speaking with your professors, and/or consulting with your family and friends. Regardless of the route you take to finding applied experience in your desired field, know that these types of opportunities are not going to fall in your lap. Instead, you have to work hard and take the initiative to make things happen. Oh, and are you too busy to do this during school? A lot of the people I know who got internships in college were busy during the school year too. Guess what they did? That's right, they got their experience in the summer.

SO WHAT?

I know that it will be easy for you to read this chapter and agree with what I wrote and then toss the book into the trash as soon as you are not being held accountable for reading it. Don't do that. Instead, think about how you can utilize the material in this chapter in your life and then take the time to learn the skills and gain the experience you need to become a successful professional. This is important because while earning a degree is a great accomplishment, it is not enough to land you a job. Just because you graduate from college does not mean you will find gainful employment. No, if you want to increase your chances of getting a job once you graduate you have to make sure you take the time to cultivate the skills and gain the experience employers are looking for. Remember, you are not entitled to anything in life. So be sure you do what it takes to earn what you want.

In human relationships there are three types of commitments: the commitments you have to honor, the commitments you ought to honor, and the commitments you want to honor.[39] "Have to" commitments are those where you legitimately have to do something. For example, if you are in jail you have to do what your captors tell you to do. "Ought to" commitments are those you should honor. These are commitments to things such as promises you make friends and responsibilities you accept as an adult. The third type, the "want to" commitment, is something you choose to do. Examples of this type of commitment are reflected in long-term bonds with a romantic partner. Know this, unless you are physically being held prisoner, the only thing you ever *have* to do is die. That's it, that's it, THAT IS IT! For everything else there is a choice. In this section of the book I am trying to tell you what you ought to do if you expect to succeed in college and beyond. Of course, you do not have to do what I recommend and I cannot make you want to do it. Doing well is your job and, as the old cliché goes, you can lead a horse to water but you cannot make it drink. In this case, you are the horse and it is up to you to drink. That just happened.

THE FUTURE OF YOU

Just because you believe does not necessarily mean that you will achieve. Dreams don't come true for people every day. If you want to reach your goals in life you are going to have to do something about it. Take some time now to outline a plan of action.

On the following pages I have a few lines with some numbers on them. This is what I want you to do: 1) Think of three goals you have for yourself either academically or professionally (or both) and write them down. Try to be as specific as possible so that you can come back to this book at some point and see if you actually achieved what you set out to do. 2) Write down the behaviors that you need to perform to get to where you want. Again, the more specific you are the better. Come up with a plan of action that will help you articulate the daily activities you need carry out in order to reach the goals you cited in Section 1. Although your goals and the steps you take to achieve them may change from time to time, this is a good place for you to start. 3) Finally, I want you to write down the names of three people you can have conversations with regarding the type of future you want. Then, next to those names write out a list of questions you can ask to help you learn about the steps you need to take to get to your final destination.

My students often tell me that they like interaction in our class lectures and that they like activities that are hands-on. So far in this book I have done all the creating. Now it's your turn to participate by completing the exercise. It is important that you do this because scientists know that you are more likely to follow through with your intentions and achieve your goals if you take the time to plan your future.[40] Moreover, there is a saying that goes something like this: "The journey of a thousand miles starts with the first step." You are at the first step. And, for you to get to where you want to be at the end of your thousand-mile journey, it is important that you start walking in the right direction. That means doing what it takes to achieve your goals, *now*. So, do the exercise.

THE FUTURE OF YOU—EXERCISE

1) _____
  _____
  _____
  _____
  _____
  _____
  _____
  _____
  _____
  _____
  _____
  _____
  _____
  _____
  _____
  _____
  _____
  _____
  _____
  _____
  _____
  _____
  _____

2) _____
_____
_____
_____
_____
_____
_____
_____
_____
_____
_____
_____
_____
_____
_____
_____
_____
_____
_____
_____
_____
_____
_____
_____

3) _____

CONCLUSION

CONCLUSION

You finished reading the book. Good for you. Seriously, good for you. Now put what you learned into practice. Then, treat yourself and YouTube "Chocolate Rain" by Tay Zonday.

Think back to the beginning of this book and about how I told you that college is not for everyone. I stand by that statement. After reading this book you may come to find that you are not cut out for doing well in a college environment. That is OK. I am sure there are plenty of things you can do well and I know that you can be very successful without a bachelor's degree. Still, for many of you going to college is the right thing to do.

That said, if you are dedicated to going to college then I suggest that you also dedicate yourself to doing it right. And now that you have read the book you should feel confident in your abilities to do just that. But just because you have the skills to perform a task does not mean that you will be able to do it. You also need motivation. For some people who read this book it is going to take a major change in lifestyle to follow my prescriptions.

For others, it will not be too difficult to do what I recommend. Either way, it is important for you to decide what you want to get out of college and then work hard to achieve it. In about four or five years you *will* be done with school. And, when people ask you what you learned or what you want to do with your life you should have some concrete answers. Sure, school is meant to be fun. And sure, you will have a lot of important social experiences while at your university. But two major reasons you are in college are to get a job and to learn information that will help you in your career. Never forget that.

Never forget what you learned in this book either. After reading this book you now know why a variety of myths about college are not true. In place of those myths you have a view of reality from a professor's standpoint. Components of that reality include the facts that you are solely responsible for your grades; college professors reward excellence, not effort; professors want you to do well; you help create the classroom atmosphere; professors are like you; professors do not like handing out bad grades or tormenting you with criticism; you need to do assignments the right way; not everyone will get an A; professors do not give tests "just because"; professors won't hold your hand in class; you need to manage your time to be productive while in school; and not all professors will be teaching ninjas.

After reading this book you also know what it means to be an adult student. Of the many aspects cited earlier, I mentioned that it is important that you show up to class, come on time, take responsibility for your education, respect your professors, and master the basics. I know that this is commonsensical advice and that people may be aware of what it takes to be a responsible adult. However, knowing what it takes to be a responsible adult and doing what it takes to be a responsible adult are two different things. I am constantly surprised by how many unfortunate students have a hard time putting this knowledge into practice. Don't be one of them.

You also learned about communication with your professors and I taught you about our expectations regarding e-mails and office hours. Use the tools given to you in college wisely and be sure to recognize that professors are a terrific resource for your academic and professional growth.

Next, I taught you how to listen well in class. This is an important skill for you to master if you ever want to be successful in translating the material you learn in college into working knowledge. But remember, listening well doesn't simply mean that you just expose yourself to noise. No, listening includes hearing, attending, understanding, remembering, evaluating, and responding. Moreover, all of this has to occur while you battle a variety of noise and deal with flaws inherent in the human communication process.

I also taught you a few things about studying for exams. To earn A's on tests you learned that you need to have accurate information, memorize the material, and have learned the material so well that you can teach someone else. I also gave you a few tips regarding how to study strategically. Doing well on your tests will not be an easy thing to do but, then again, nobody said college would be easy.

Finally, I ended this book by talking to you about how to choose a major and explaining what employers look for in college graduates. In essence, I wanted to communicate the importance of having goals while in college and that you need to use your time to prepare yourself to achieve these goals. Instead of thinking that your career will begin once you graduate, I want you to realize that college is the first step in your career. In many ways, your career starts the first moment you step onto campus.

So, that's it! The book is done! Yay! Good for you! However, just because the book is done does not mean that you should be done with the book. As I mentioned in the section referring to studying for tests, you need to read something more than once if you want to be able to recall it. I know that if you are this far along in the book you more than likely learned a few things. But information and advice are only useful if you can remember to use them. Keep this book with you and refer back to it from time to time. If you can utilize the information presented in it then I promise that your academic life will be a very successful one.

Good luck! And if you ever want to chat about anything in this book feel free to contact me directly at sanbolkan@gmail. com. Or you can even try your luck Facebook-befriending me. Just, when you friend-request me, be sure to reference this book ... I do not add random strangers. Make it happen!

REFERENCES

REFERENCES

1. Goodboy, A. K., and Bolkan, S. "College teacher misbehaviors: Direct and indirect effects on student communication behavior and traditional learning outcomes." *Western Journal of Communication* (2009) 73, 204–219.

2. Ericsson, K. A., Krampe, R. T., and Tesch-Romer, C. "The role of deliberate practice in the acquisition of expert performance." *Psychological Review* (1993) 100, 363–406.

3. Day, J. C., and Newburger, E. C. "The big payoff: Educational attainment and synthetic estimates of work-life earnings." U.S. Census Bureau, 2002.

4. Sabatelli, R. M. "The marital comparison level index: A measure for assessing outcome related to expectations." *Journal of Marriage and the Family* (1984) 46, 651–662.

5. Kruger, J., Wirtz, D., Van Boven, L., and Altermatt, T. W. "The effort heuristic." *Journal of Experimental Social Psychology* (2004) 40, 91–98.

6. Eiszler, C. F. "College students' evaluations of teaching and grade inflation." *Research in Higher Education* (2002) 43, 483–501.

7. Bloomsburg University: Office of the Registrar. "Grades and GPA." 2010. (Accessed April 25, 2010) http://www.bloomu.edu/registrar/grades.php

8. University of California, Los Angeles: Registrar's office. "General catalog." 2009–2010. (Accessed April 25, 2010) http://www.registrar.ucla.edu/archive/catalog/2009-10/uclageneralcatalog09-10.pdf

9. St. Edward's University. "Undergraduate bulletin." 2009–2010. (Accessed April 25, 2010) http://www.stedwards.edu/dasx/09-10_Undergrad_Bulletin_vs2%20copy.pdf

10. "Final course grades, grading procedures, and final assessments." 2010. (Accessed April 25, 2010) http://www.csulb.edu/divisions/aa/grad_undergrad/senate/documents/policy/2005/07/

11. Severin, W. J., and Tankard, J. W. Jr. 2001. *Communication theories: Origins, methods, and uses in the mass media.* New York: Addison Wesley Longman, Inc.

12. Alicke, M. D. "Global self-evaluation as determined by the desirability and controllability of trait adjectives." *Journal of Personality and Social Psychology* (1985) 49, 1621–1630.

Alicke, M. D., Klotz, M. L., Breitenbecher, D. L., Yurak, T. J., and Vredenburg, D. S. "Personal contact, individuation, and the better-than-average effect." *Journal of Personality and Social Psychology* (1995) 68, 804–825.

Shore, T. H., Shore, L. M., and Thornton, G. C. "Construct validity of self- and peer evaluations of performance dimensions in an assessment center." *Journal of Applied Psychology* (1992) 77, 42–54.

Suls, J., Lemos, K., and Lockett, S. H. "Self-esteem, construal, and comparisons with the self, friends, and peers." *Journal of Personality and Social Psychology* (2002) 82, 252–261.

13. Eberhardt, B. J., McGee, P., and Moser, S. "Business concerns regarding MBA education: Effects on recruiting." *Journal of Education for Business* (1997) 72, 293–296.

14. Mischel, W., Shoda, Y., and Rodriguez, M. L. "Delay of gratification in children." *Science* (1989) 244, 933–938.

15. Bolkan, S., and Goodboy, A. K. "Behavioral indicators of transformational leadership in the college classroom." Paper presented to the National Communication Association, Chicago, IL, 2009.

Bolkan, S., and Goodboy, A. K. "Transformational leadership in the classroom: Fostering student learning, student participation, and teacher credibility." *Journal of Instructional Psychology* (2009) 36, 1–11.

Goodboy, A. K., and Bolkan, S. "College teacher misbehaviors: Direct and indirect effects on student communication behavior and traditional learning outcomes." *Western Journal of Communication* (2009) 73, 204–219.

16. Kearney, P., Plax, T. G., Hays, L. R., and Ivey, M. J. "College teacher misbehaviors: What students don't like about what teachers say or do." *Communication Quarterly* (1991) 39, 309–324.

17. Romer, D. "Do students go to class? Should they?" *Journal of Economic Perspectives* (1993) 7, 167–174.

Van Blerkom, M. L. "Academic perseverance, class attendance, and performance in the college classroom." Paper presented at the annual Meeting of the American Psychological Association, Toronto, Ontario, Canada, 1996.

18. Jones, E. E., and Nisbett, R. E. "The actor observer: Divergent perceptions of the causes of behavior," in *Attribution: Perceiving the causes of behavior*, edited by E. E. Jones, D. E. Kanouse, H. H. Kelley, R. E. Nisbett, S. Valins, and B. Weiner (Morristown, NJ: General Learning Press, 1971), 79–94.

19. Kelley, H. H. "The process of causal attribution." *American Psychologist* (1973) 28, 107–128.

20. Lefcourt, H. M. 1976. *Locus of control: Current trends in theory and research.* Hillsdale, NJ: Erlbaum.

21. Rotter, J. B. 1954. *Social learning and clinical psychology.* New York: Prentice-Hall.

22. Burgoon, J. K., Dunbar, N. E., and Segrin, C. "Nonverbal influence," in *The persuasion handbook: Developments in theory and practice,* edited by J. P. Dillard and M. Pfau (Thousand Oaks, CA: Sage, 2002), 445–473.

23. Bolkan, S., and Daly, J. A. "Organizational responses to consumer complaints: A re-examination of the impact of organizational messages in response to service and product-based failures." *Journal of Consumer Satisfaction, Dissatisfaction & Complaining Behavior* (2008) 21, 1–22.

    Bolkan, S., and Daly, J. A. "Organizational responses to consumer complaints: An approach to understanding the effectiveness of remedial accounts." *Journal of Applied Communication Research* (2009) 37, 21–39.

24. Conlon, D. E., and Murray, N. M. "Customer perceptions of corporate responses to product complaints: The role of explanations." *Academy of Management Journal* (1996) 39, 1040–1056.

25. Coser, L. A. 1967. *Continuities in the study of social conflict.* New York: Free Press.
    Simmel, G. 1953. *Conflict and the web of group affiliations.* Translated by K. H. Wolff. New York: Free Press.

26. Galvin, K. M., Bylund, C. L., and Brommel, B. J. 2007. *Family communication: Cohesion and change*. Boston, MA: Allyn and Bacon.

27. Wilmot, W. W., and Hocker, J. L. 2005. *Interpersonal conflict*. Boston, MA: McGraw-Hill.

28. Deci, E. L., and Ryan, R. M. "The 'what' and 'why' of goal pursuits: Human needs and the self-determination of behavior." *Psychological Inquiry* (2000) 11, 227–268.

29. Spitzberg, B. H., and Cupach, W. R. 1984. *Interpersonal communication competence*. Beverly Hills, CA: Sage.

30. Stephens, K. K., Houser, M. L., and Cowan, R. L. "R U able to meat me: The impact of students' overly casual email messages to instructors." *Communication Education* (2009) 58, 303–326.

31. Stephens, K. K., Houser, M. L., and Cowan, R. L. "R U able to meat me: The impact of students' overly casual email messages to instructors." *Communication Education* (2009) 58, 303–326.

31. Knapp, M. L., and Vangelisti, A. L. 2005. *Interpersonal communication and human relationships*. Boston: Allyn and Bacon.

32. Guerrero, L. K., Andersen, P. A., and Afifi, W. A. 2007. *Close encounters: Communication in relationships*. Los Angeles: Sage.

Knapp, M. L., and Vangelisti, A. L. 2005. *Interpersonal communication and human relationships*. Boston: Allyn and Bacon.

33. Brewer, W. F., and Treyens, J. C. "Role of schemata in memory for places." *Cognitive Psychology* (1981) 13, 207–230.

34. McIntosh, D. N. "Facial feedback hypothesis: Evidence, implications, and directions." *Motivation and Emotion* (1996) 20, 121–147.

35. Greene, R. L. "Spacing effects in memory: Evidence for a two-process account." *Journal of Experimental Psychology: Learning, Memory, and Cognition* (1989) 15, 371–377.

36. McDougall, C. 2009. *Born to run: A hidden tribe, superathletes, and the greatest race the world has never seen.* New York: Knopf.

37. Eberhardt, B. J., McGee, P., and Moser, S. "Business concerns regarding MBA education: Effects on recruiting." *Journal of Education for Business* (1997) 72, 293–296.

38. Dierdorff, E. C., and Rubin, R. S. "Toward a comprehensive empirical model of managerial competencies." Project technical report presented to the MER Institute of the Graduate Management Admission Council, McLean, VA., 2006.

39. Knapp, M. L., and Vangelisti, A. L. 2005. *Interpersonal communication and human relationships.* Boston: Allyn and Bacon.

40. Norman, P., and Conner, M. "The theory of planned behavior and exercise: Evidence for the mediating and moderating roles of planning on intention-behavior relationships." *Journal of Sport and Exercise Psychology* (2005) 27, 488–504.

CPSIA information can be obtained at www.ICGtesting.com
Printed in the USA
LVOW12s0838030115

421258LV00001B/1/P